La cocina
VASCA

La cocina
VASCA

RECIPES & TRADITIONS
OF THE SPANISH
BASQUE COUNTRY

MARÍA JOSÉ SEVILLA

PHOTOGRAPHY BY CLARE WINFIELD

RYLAND PETERS & SMALL
LONDON • NEW YORK

To Pedro Subijana, a chef of chefs,
a friend I admire and love.

Senior Designer Megan Smith
Senior Editor Abi Waters
Production Manager Gordana Simakovic
Creative Director Leslie Harrington
Editorial Director Julia Charles

Food Stylist Kathy Kordalis
Prop Stylist Max Robinson
Illustrator Lyndon Hayes
Picture Researcher Jess Walton
Indexer Hilary Bird

First published in 2025 by
Ryland Peters & Small
20–21 Jockey's Fields, London
WC1R 4BW
and
1452 Davis Bugg Road
Warrenton, NC 27589

10 9 8 7 6 5 4 3 2 1

Text © María José Sevilla 2025
Illustrations © Ryland Peters & Small
2025
Design and commissioned photography
© Ryland Peters & Small 2025
(see page 192 for full picture credits)

Printed in China

ISBN: 978-1-78879-677-4

A CIP record for this book is available
from the British Library. US Library
of Congress cataloging-in-Publication
Data has been applied for.

NOTES
· All spoon measurements are level
unless otherwise specified 5 ml =
1 teaspoon, 15 ml = 1 tablespoon
· Uncooked or partially cooked eggs
should not be served to the very old,
frail, young children, pregnant women
or those with compromised immune
systems.
· When a recipe calls for the grated
zest of citrus fruit, buy unwaxed
fruit and wash well before using.
· Ovens should be preheated to
the specified temperatures.
· To sterilize preserving jars, wash
them in hot, soapy water and rinse
in boiling water. Place in a large
saucepan and cover with hot water.
With the saucepan lid on, bring the
water to the boil and continue boiling
for 15 minutes. Turn off the heat and
leave the jars in the hot water until just
before they are to be filled. Invert the
jars onto a clean dish towel to dry.
Sterilize the lids for 5 minutes, by
boiling (remove any rubber seals first).
Jars should be filled and sealed while
they are still hot.

Contents

Introduction

My fascination with Basque food started early. My grandmother, Silvia, was a professional cook from Navarra who often prepared traditional Basque dishes while staying with us in Madrid. What I did not know at that time was how immersed I would become in all things Basque. My involvement began in the mid-1980s when I was asked to organise a lunch in London for the British press. The event was to celebrate the achievements of a revolutionary new Basque food movement known as the *La Nueva Cocina Vasca* (New Basque Cuisine). This movement was started by a group of young Basque chefs in the 1970s. It aimed to update *La Cocina Vasca* (Traditional Basque Cooking) and marked the beginning of a remarkable success, placing creative Spanish professional kitchens on the world map.

Since the nineteenth century, *La Cocina Vasca* has been divided into two categories: *La Cocina de Siempre*, Basque traditional food prepared at home and in popular restaurants, and *La Alta Cocina*, fine dining greatly influenced by French cooking. By the 1980s, this had already changed. Travelling up and down the country, talking to chefs and home cooks, visiting local markets and, most importantly, tasting dishes, I realised how Basque food, both traditional and reinvented, coexisted in harmony.

Having eventually found the right chef and the right menu, I discovered a history that fired my imagination, inviting me to go further. The menu written for the lunch was going to include a dessert made with apples, puff pastry and *Mamia*. '*Mamia*?' I asked the chef. '*Mamia*,' he said, 'is a sheep's milk delicacy that in some *caseríos* (traditional farmhouses) in northern Navarra is still prepared in the old-fashioned way, using a large traditional wooden pitcher carved out of one solid piece of wood. This utensil has always been known as a *kaiku* and has a long and interesting history associated with the ancient world of the Basques.' By then I was intrigued and started looking for answers. I researched and published a paper on the *kaiku*, then wrote my first book about the special relationship between Basques and food, which in my opinion is without comparison elsewhere in the world.

Who are the Basques? I asked myself. Where do they live? What language do they speak? Where does their intense love of food come from and, equally important, how is Basque food enjoyed and how has such a great reputation been established everywhere within the Iberian Peninsula?

While my area of research on this subject has always been based in Euskadi as Basque Spain is known – Vizcaya, Guipúzcoa, Alava and parts of Navarra – the land of the Basques, Euskal Herria, actually continues much further along the coast, right through to the Pyrenees and into the French provinces of Lower Navarre, Labourd and Soule. This is the reason why I have included several French Basque recipes in this book.

All Basques speak a very ancient language called Euskera. They all share a passion for food, which brings me to my next question: where does the excellent reputation that Basque food enjoys come from? Even today, when wonderful food can be enjoyed all over Spain, ask any Spaniard where you will find the best food in the country and they will most likely say in the north, in the Basque Country. Basques are serious about their culinary traditions, which they respect and follow with passion. (I am not including the new passion for innovative food that is highly impressive but does require skill and a level of professional expertise.)

Basques believe in quality as much as quantity. They are very dedicated when preparing and tasting their delicious dishes, seeking a perfect harmony between people and food to the point where others

might think it has become almost an obsession. Virtually all Basques are good cooks, or they aspire to be. I believe that they are born already inspired. They simply love their cooking, as much as to please themselves as to please others. Whether in a bar or restaurant with friends or at home with family, they love to share delicious food whenever possible. In the Basque Country, there are thousands of eating places to choose from, where the quality of the food and the wine (or cider) they love so dearly is guaranteed.

A few years ago, I wrote some words on the Basque passion for cooking and food. Even if the world has changed since then, I believe those words are still valid, I have just added a few more: 'If I close my eyes to conjure up a scene of Basque cooking, it takes the shape of an earthenware pot, cooking either on a farmhouse range, on a spectacular stove in a *txokos* (men's gastronomic society) or in the ultra-modern kitchen of one of the best restaurants in the world. The first is tended by a woman, the second by a man and the third by both men and women.'

Thinking about those words in preparation for this book, I travelled again to Gernika, in Vizcaya and to the locality of Astigarraga in Guipúzcoa. I stopped in Bilbao before travelling to the city of San Sebastián and then on to the town of Biarritz in the Basque part of France, before returning to London.

Not far from Gernika, I visited the *caserío* of my friend Luisa Aulestia. Talking to Luisa, I realised that even if life in the Basque *caserío* has changed dramatically since I first met her in the 1980s, she was still in charge of the house, the kitchen, the chickens, a few ducks and the two pigs while her husband still cooks in the local *txokos* from time to time.

In Luisa's vegetable garden, which is her pride and joy, she plants black and white beans, climbing towards the sun, supported not by bean poles but by sweetcorn/maize plants, as the Aztecs and Mayas did centuries before her. She is still growing her potatoes and amazingly large cabbages, which she calls *berza*. In the right season, bottling tomatoes and drying peppers and chillies/chiles has always been a priority for Luisa. She hangs red *choricero* and hot *guindilla* peppers from the windows to dry and bottles the fresh green *piparras* chillies, which all the family love. Come autumn/fall, from the apple orchards that surround the house, her husband and son make their own cider, which I was delighted to taste before lunch. She served *alubias negras de Tolosa* (black bean stew with black pudding/blood sausage and cabbage), accompanied by a small plate of *piparras* and, as is the custom, a glass of red wine from the Rioja Alavesa, an area of wine production inside Euskadi.

The following day, as I travelled towards the border with France, I stopped first in Astigarraga at the *sidreras* (cider house) of another friend, Rosario, whose recipes I love to cook. Astigarraga is a town in Guipúzcoa, well known for cider and cider houses. As I arrived, Rosario was upstairs in the main kitchen preparing one of her renowned *tortillas de bacalao* (omelette with salted cod) with properly desalted fish, large spring onions/scallions and green (bell) peppers, while her brother was already downstairs grilling the *chuletas* (T-bone steaks) in front of diners.

On the move again, I reached the ever charming San Sebastián where I found accommodation not far from the popular La Parte Vieja in the heart of the city. From eleven o'clock every day, La Parte Vieja is full of locals and tourists enjoying a *pintxo*, a little dish with the tastiest tomatoes or a wonderful plate of mushrooms. Mmm... My mouth is watering just remembering this scene. Walking down the streets, I could see the open front door of one of the best-known *txokos* in town. I could not resist stopping and sneaking into the main room, which was empty. I knew that come lunch or dinner time, a number of friends (usually all male members of the gastronomic society) would be sitting, waiting for the one member who had been cooking for hours during the morning

to serve the food, possibly *arroz con almejas* (rice with clams) and *merluza en salsa verde* (hake in parsley sauce) cooked in a *cazuela* (earthenware pot). Not so long ago, women were not allowed to enter these societies. Now things have changed somewhat. Women are now invited on certain days to join their husbands or friends for lunch or dinner, but they are still not allowed to cook. Gastronomic societies were created as male-only clubs, considered by their members as a refuge to cook and eat for their own pleasure and for that of other members, some of whom are acclaimed chefs. It is a space chefs can disappear to from time to time, where they can experience dishes closer to home cooking that they may never confess to in public!

Whether they have a Michelin star or not, in the whole of the Basque Country, chefs are rightly considered brilliant stars themselves. Around the city of San Sebastián, there are 16 restaurants with Michelin stars: Akelarre, Arzak and Martín Berasategui have three stars each, making this a great reason to spend my very last evening there. I sampled some truly wonderful dishes (too many to remember) that have earned this city its reputation as a world-acclaimed food paradise. So here I was, heading up to the Monte Igueldo where Akelarre looks down onto one of the most beautiful bays that I have ever seen. Chef Pedro Subijana, a brilliant chef who I was privileged to accompany during his visit to London in the 1980s, was still the chef patron in San Sebastián.

The following morning in Biarritz, across the border in France, I had time to stop at an excellent pâtisserie (pastry shop) to buy the classic *gâteau Basque*, filled with cherries, which I took back to London with me. Later, in a small restaurant close to the airport, not far from the sea and imposing Pyrenees, I had for lunch a full plate of *ttoro*, the famous Basque fish and shellfish stew. I knew I had to return to the Basque Country as soon as possible.

HOMEMADE BASIC STOCKS

Caldo de pollo
CHICKEN STOCK

The aroma of chicken stock brings back memories of my mother's kitchen. The stock was used in so many dishes: soups, casseroles and croquetas (croquettes), which I am still making today. Here, I have included a simple stock recipe, yet to me, it is the most pure in taste; beautifully clear and with no unnecessary ingredients to hide behind. It is made with fresh chicken bones, vegetables, herbs, black peppercorns and plenty of water.

2 fresh chicken carcasses
2 carrots, peeled and roughly chopped
2 celery leaves
2–3 tablespoons apple cider vinegar
1 bouquet garni (made with parsley sprigs,
    thyme sprigs and 2 bay leaves)
7 whole black peppercorns
salt, to taste

MAKES 2 LITRES/QUARTS

Place all the ingredients (except the salt) in a large stock pot and pour over enough water to cover them completely. Place over a medium to high heat and bring to a rapid simmer. Skim off any foam that appears on the surface; keep doing this until the stock stays clear. Keeping the heat low, gently simmer the stock for about 3 hours or until reduced by one-third. Leave the stock to cool, then strain through a fine-mesh sieve/strainer. Adjust the seasoning with salt to taste. Use the quantity needed for your recipe, then you can store the remaining stock in the fridge for a few days or in the freezer in portions for up to 3 months.

Caldo de carne
MEAT STOCK

Home cooks can use ready-prepared, store-bought meat and bone stocks, but making a stock at home from fresh ingredients is an easy thing to do. Yes, it takes time, but the result is better for recipes and as has been demonstrated by dieticians as being much healthier.

1 kg/2¼ lb. inexpensive cuts of meat,
    such as oxtail, beef shank or shin
2 kg/4½ lb. fresh beef bones
1 onion, peeled and halved
2 carrots, peeled and roughly chopped
1 celery stick/rib
salt, to taste

MAKES 2 LITRES/QUARTS

Place all the ingredients (except the salt) in a large stock pot and pour over 5 litres/quarts water to cover them completely. Place over a medium to high heat and bring to a boil. Skim off any foam that appears on the surface; keep doing this until the stock stays clear. Keeping the heat low, gently simmer the stock for at least 2½ hours or until reduced by at least half. Leave the stock to cool, then strain through a fine-mesh sieve/strainer. Adjust the seasoning with salt to taste. Use the quantity needed for your recipe, then you can store the stock in the fridge for a few days or in the freezer in portions for up to 3 months.

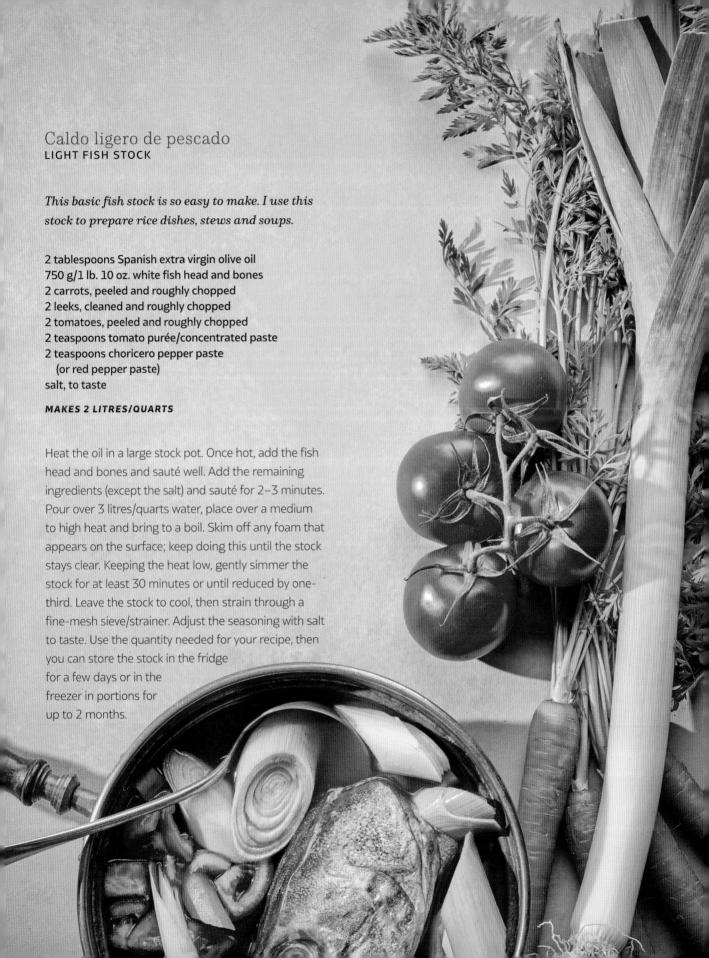

Caldo ligero de pescado
LIGHT FISH STOCK

This basic fish stock is so easy to make. I use this stock to prepare rice dishes, stews and soups.

2 tablespoons Spanish extra virgin olive oil
750 g/1 lb. 10 oz. white fish head and bones
2 carrots, peeled and roughly chopped
2 leeks, cleaned and roughly chopped
2 tomatoes, peeled and roughly chopped
2 teaspoons tomato purée/concentrated paste
2 teaspoons choricero pepper paste
   (or red pepper paste)
salt, to taste

MAKES 2 LITRES/QUARTS

Heat the oil in a large stock pot. Once hot, add the fish head and bones and sauté well. Add the remaining ingredients (except the salt) and sauté for 2–3 minutes. Pour over 3 litres/quarts water, place over a medium to high heat and bring to a boil. Skim off any foam that appears on the surface; keep doing this until the stock stays clear. Keeping the heat low, gently simmer the stock for at least 30 minutes or until reduced by one-third. Leave the stock to cool, then strain through a fine-mesh sieve/strainer. Adjust the seasoning with salt to taste. Use the quantity needed for your recipe, then you can store the stock in the fridge for a few days or in the freezer in portions for up to 2 months.

PINTXOS

Small & delicious bite-size snacks

Pintxos: A way of living

Even if they appear to be similar in some respects, a *pintxo* is neither a *tapa* nor a *ración*, which is a larger portion of a *tapa*. Both *tapas* and *pintxos* are associated with an informal way of eating while drinking wine or beer in bars and restaurants. *Tapa* comes from *tapar*, the verb meaning 'to cover' that was originally used in Andalucía. A glass of Fino or Manzanilla sherry would be covered with something delicious, such as a small slice of Serrano ham. *Pintxo* is a Basque word derived from the Castilian *pinchar*, meaning 'to prick'. In general terms, *pintxo* is the name given in the Basque Country to a small portion of food skewered on a wooden cocktail stick/toothpick. Nowadays, *pintxos* have become much more complex than that.

Pintxos are a constantly evolving, original food adventure prepared in a variety of shapes and sizes using an array of quality ingredients. They are presented in the most attractive way imaginable, visibly displayed on counters to attract passers-by. Even if many *pintxo* shapes appear to be similar, their diversity is astonishing. Some are prepared on slices of the local bread, while others are offered in pastry cases known as *tartaletas* (tartlets). You can also find *medias noches* (midnight buns), which are small, slightly sweet buns filled with cheese and smoked ham or other delights. Equally good are the family of minute sweet and salty croissants, which I love. Some *pintxos* are held together by a cocktail stick, some others are not, and the variety is growing by the day. On my last visit to San Sebastián, in a popular modern bar, I had a spectacular small plate of rice cooked to complete perfection. It was prepared with a clam sauce so delicious that I felt compelled to ask for a second helping. I was determined not to leave a single grain behind.

Perhaps surprisingly, some *pintxos* are now quite sweet. At La Viña, the renowned bar in San Sebastián,

they offer as a *pintxo* a piece of the iconic burnt cheesecake that has made this bar one of the most popular in the old city. Foreign visitors adore it.

Many *pintxos* are prepared in advance, but never too long beforehand. Freshness is paramount. For me, it is the hot *pintxo* made on demand that I have become fascinated by, perhaps not surprisingly. Today more than ever, healthy competition encourages chefs to dedicate their professional lives to what has become the amazing *cocina Vasca en miniatura* (Basque cuisine in miniature).

Of course, we are talking about the Basque Country here. Since the 1980s, the innovation and creativity in Spanish food, and the influence of the dishes prepared by talented Basque chefs of all ages, has revolutionised bars and restaurants not only in San Sebastián, birthplace of the *pintxo*, but all over the Basque Country and the rest of Spain.

While socialising in bars, Basques drink cider and beer. They drink red wine mostly from Rioja and Navarra and, of course, the delightfully fresh and slightly acidic *txakoli* white wine produced in the areas of Orduña and Orozko in Vizcaya and on the hilly slopes of Getaria, in Guipúzcoa.

Clockwise from top left: La Viña in San Sebastián; temping pintxos on a counter; La Concha, an iconic Basque beach; vines near Artomaña; Plaza de la Constitución, San Sebastián. Overleaf: Txakoli vineyards overlooking the Cantabrian Sea in Getaria.

Gildas y piparras

ANCHOVY, OLIVE & PIPARRAS CHILLI SKEWERS

The original Gilda – one of the most popular pintxos – is a banderilla, the Castilian name given to a wooden cocktail stick/toothpick used to spear various ingredients. Gildas have only three elements: anchovies, green olives and piparras (moderately hot preserved green chillies/chiles). The anchovies used in Gildas are cured in salt, rinsed, covered in olive oil and then canned. They are pure umami.

Today, Gildas are found in many bars all over the Basque Country, but it is Casa Vallés, a classic bar in San Sebastián, where it is believed that this delicious banderilla was first created in the 1970s. Apparently it was to celebrate the film Gilda, which was showing at local cinemas at the time.

In the last few years, bars have been serving fresh piparras from June to October. Fried in plenty of olive oil until tender and sprinkled with coarse sea salt, they are served piping hot. On their own, piparras are simply wonderful.

12 good-quality anchovy fillets canned in olive oil (see note below)

12 green olives (see note below), stoned/pitted

12 piparras chillies/chiles (see note below), halved

12 wooden cocktail sticks/toothpicks

MAKES 12

Thread one end of an anchovy fillet onto a cocktail stick/toothpick. Next, spear an olive with the stick, followed by a piece or two of piparra. Pass the stick through the other end of the anchovy fillet to secure, wrapping the anchovy around the other ingredients. Repeat with all the remaining anchovies, olives and piparras to make 12 skewers.

NOTES

» *Cantabria and the Basque Country produce excellent anchovies. They are expensive but their unique taste (umami at its best) makes them irresistible.*

» *I love Andalucian Gordal olives, which are fat green ones. I often marinate them in olive oil with lemon zest and rosemary sprigs.*

» *Piparras are a type of Basque green chilli/chile of moderate heat, which are preserved in vinegar and water with salt.*

Tartaletas con bechamel de setas, chalotes y langostinos

CEP & SHALLOT TARTLETS WITH PRAWNS

Tartaletas are tartlets – small pastry cases filled with an assortment of ingredients, including ensaladilla de siempre (see page 45) and smoked salmon, often in a bechamel sauce. They are normally prepared as part of a canapé tray to serve on Christmas Day or at other festivities, but they are also popular as a traditional pintxo enjoyed any day of the year.

I love to use ceps. They are expensive but quite unique. Other types of mushrooms will also do very well, though the texture and flavour of the cep is difficult to surpass.

TARTLET PASTRY CASES
240 g/1¾ cups plain/all-purpose flour
30 g/⅓ cup ground almonds
20 g/¾ oz. icing/confectioner's sugar
120 g/½ cup cold unsalted butter
2 g/½ teaspoon salt
1 medium/US large egg

CEP & SHALLOT FILLING
45 g/3 tablespoons unsalted butter
1 or 2 shallots, peeled and finely
    chopped
1 large cep, cleaned and thinly sliced
2 tablespoons plain/all-purpose flour
400 ml/1¾ cups full-fat/whole milk,
    or as needed
pinch of freshly grated nutmeg
salt and ground white pepper

TO FINISH
1 tablespoon olive oil
12 raw prawns/shrimp, deveined
    and peeled
pinch of finely chopped flat-leaf parsley

*12 individual tartlet tins, 6 cm/2½ inches
    diameter, 3 cm/1¼ inches deep*

8-cm/3-inch round cookie cutter

MAKES 12

First, prepare the pastry. Place all the ingredients (except the egg), in the bowl of a food processor and mix on a medium speed. When the texture is grainy (this will take around 4 minutes), gradually add the egg. Continue mixing at the same speed until all the ingredients are fully incorporated and have formed a soft dough that does not stick to the sides of the bowl.

Place the dough on a clean work surface. Using your palms and fingers, gently form it into a ball and flatten slightly. Cover the dough with cling film/plastic wrap and pat into a square shape (this makes rolling out easier). Chill in the fridge for at least 30 minutes.

Preheat the oven to 160°C/140°C fan/325°F/Gas 3.

Unwrap the dough and cut it into two equal pieces. Place one of the halves back in the fridge. Using the other half, place the dough on a rectangular sheet of parchment paper and cover with a second sheet. Gently roll out the dough between the sheets to a thickness of about 3 mm/⅛ inch. Using the cookie cutter, punch out 6 rounds. (Gather up any excess pastry scraps, mould into a ball, wrap in cling film and store in the freezer to use later for another recipe.)

Place one pastry round inside each tartlet tin. Using the tips of your fingers, gently press the pastry into the shape of each tin, making sure the dough reaches right to the top of the mould. Using a small fork, prick all over the base of each pastry case. Place the lined tartlet tins in the fridge to chill. Repeat with the second piece of pastry dough.

Place the lined tartlet tins in the preheated oven and cook for 20 minutes or until lightly golden. Remove from the oven and leave to cool completely before removing the pastry cases from the tins.

While the pastry cases are cooking, prepare the filling. Melt the butter in a saucepan, then add the shallots and sauté until translucent. Add the cep slices and sauté until all the moisture has evaporated, they are tender and have taken on a little colour. You may need to add a little more butter.

Sprinkle the flour over the shallots and cep and stir to make a paste. Little by little, pour in the milk, stirring continuously until the paste is completely diluted and forms a smooth sauce. Add the nutmeg and season the sauce with a little salt and white pepper. Continue stirring until you can no longer taste the flour and the bechamel sauce has thickened.

Season the prawns with a pinch of salt. Warm a tablespoon of olive oil in a small frying pan/skillet. Once hot, add the prawns and cook briefly on both sides until they just turn pink. Do not overcook the prawns. Slice each prawn into two pieces.

Spoon some of the warm cep and shallot filling into each pastry case, then place the two halves of a prawn on top so they are visible. Scatter over a little finely chopped parsley. Serve warm.

Tartaletas de ensaladilla, aceituna negra y huevo hilado
CLASSIC RUSSIAN SALAD & BLACK OLIVE TARTLETS WITH EGG STRANDS

Displays of pintxos in any Basque bar are a delight for the senses. There are many different shapes and, above all, colours; the red of (bell) peppers; the pink of prawns/shrimp; the green of olives, piparras and herbs; the orange of sea urchins, the yellow of egg yolks and huevo hilado (egg strands). In Spain, you can buy huevo hilado in pâtisseries, however it is not difficult to make at home. I like to make tartlets, but this filling is equally delicious served in ready-made, store-bought vol-au-vents.

6 baked pastry cases (see page 20)
½ quantity of Ensaladilla de Siempre
    (Classic Russian Salad, see page 45)
6 black olives, stoned/pitted

EGG STRANDS
100 g/½ cup caster/superfine sugar
2 large/US extra-large egg yolks

cooking syringe

MAKES 6

First, make the egg strands. To prepare a simple syrup, dissolve the sugar in 150 ml/⅔ cup water in a saucepan. Place the pan over a low heat, then gradually increase the heat. As the water heats up, large bubbles appear on the surface followed by smaller bubbles a few minutes later. Check the density of the syrup by scooping up a spoonful and pouring it back into the pan. The syrup is ready when it just still runs off the spoon in a thin stream.

Meanwhile, fill a bowl with cold water and ice cubes. Pass the egg yolks through a fine mesh sieve/strainer into a bowl. Fill the syringe with the egg yolk. Working in a circular motion, squeeze the egg yolks into the hot syrup in continuous strands. Let the strands set in the syrup. Using a slotted spoon, carefully lift the strands out of the pan and into the iced water. Once set, transfer the strands to a clean dish cloth to dry.

Fill each pastry case generously with the salad, add a black olive on top and finish with a few egg strands.

NOTE
» *The quantities given are for a small amount of huevo hilado (egg strands). You can make more, if you prefer, as they keep well in the fridge for a few days.*

Pintxo de champignon, mermelada de cebolla roja y torreznos

MUSHROOMS WITH RED ONION MARMALADE & PORK CRACKLING

One of the most wonderful things about pintxos is that they allow us to showcase our culinary creativity and pair ingredients that work well together. Following this line of thought, this pintxos includes torreznos (pork crackling) – a treat my mother used to prepare to serve with drinks. Torreznos are made from panceta curada (cured pork belly, see opposite). I have seen them used in a number of recipes and so I decided to include torreznos in this delicious pintxo, both broken into small pieces and crushed into a coarse crumbs. Even the most demanding members of my family approve!

Note that you will need to prepare the onion marmalade well in advance and the torreznos (pork crackling) 45 minutes before serving.

2 tablespoons light Spanish olive oil
or sunflower oil
4 medium and 4 small mushrooms,
cleaned and stalks removed
4 teaspoons red onion marmalade
(see below)
6 small torreznos (pork crackling, see
opposite), 4 broken into small pieces
and 2 crushed into a coarse crumbs
salt and freshly ground black pepper

RED ONION MARMALADE
500 g/1 lb. 2 oz. red onions, peeled and
thinly sliced
100 ml/⅓ cup red wine vinegar
splash of sherry vinegar
220 g/generous 1 cup brown sugar
splash of Pedro Ximénez sherry
(optional)

4 wooden cocktail sticks/toothpicks

MAKES 4

First, make the red onion marmalade. Place the sliced onions in a colander, rinse them under cold running water and then pat dry with paper towels.

Place the onions in a bowl with the red wine vinegar and sherry vinegar. Cover the bowl and leave the onions to marinate for 2–3 hours, stirring every 30 minutes. Next, add the sugar, mix well and leave to rest for a further 2 hours. The onions will become soft and turn darker in colour.

Place the onions in a saucepan and cook over a low heat for 35–40 minutes, stirring often. If you find the marmalade needs a little more sweetness, add a splash of sherry. Set aside the quantity of marmalade needed for this recipe, then transfer the rest to sterilised glass jars and seal them tightly.

To assemble the pintxos, heat 2 tablespoons olive oil in a saucepan. Place all the mushrooms in the pan in a single layer, gill sides up, and cook they are until slightly tender and have taken on some colour. Do not turn the mushrooms more than once. Season with salt and pepper. Transfer the mushrooms to paper towels.

Fill each medium-sized mushroom with a teaspoon of the red onion marmalade and a small piece of pork crackling. Top each one with a small mushroom, then scatter over the coarsely crushed pork crackling. Spear each pintxos with a cocktail stick/toothpick to secure.

NOTES

» *The red onion marmalade can be prepared well in advance of assembling the pintxos and stored in a sealed jar.*

» *The pork belly takes several days to cure, if you are making it yourself. It must then be made into pork crackling about 45 minutes before assembling the pintxos, and kept warm.*

Torreznos de panceta curada
PORK CRACKLING

A classic recipe from central Spain, also known in Andalucía and Latin America as chicharrones. Made from cured pork belly, torreznos are utterly delicious. They can be cooked in the oven, but for me, the perfect torreznos have to be deep-fried. Panceta curada can be found in Spanish delicatessens, however you can easily cure your own pork belly. It requires a piece with perfect skin, some paprika, a little salt and a few days.

500 g/1 lb. 2 oz. pork belly (ask your butcher
   to cut a piece of equal thickness all over)
1 teaspoon sweet smoked paprika
pinch of fine sea salt
sunflower oil, for frying

MAKES 500G/1 LB. 2 OZ.

To cure the meat, rub the paprika all over the pork belly, adding a few drops of water if needed. The pork will take on an attractive orange colour. Sprinkle a little salt over the pork; do not use too much as it should not be too salty. Hang the pork in a place that is neither too cold nor too warm (20°C/68°F is ideal) for 3–4 days to cure, or until the skin has dried out completely and become harder.

Cut the pork belly lengthways into four strips, each about 4 cm/1½ inches thick. (Do not cut the strips any thinner or they will curl up when fried.)

Place enough oil in a deep frying pan/skillet to cover the pork belly. Place the pork skin down in the pan while the oil is cold. Warm over a low heat and cook for about 35–40 minutes – the skin will start to crack and blister. At this point, increase the heat to high. After a few minutes, the skin of the pork will blister, puff up and become very crispy, turning into perfect crackling. Turn each piece of pork once to cook on both sides. Transfer to paper towels to absorb any excess oil. Use as directed in your recipe or serve hot, either on their own or with some bread.

Pintxo de patata, salsa alioli y escabeche casero de mejillón en vinagre de sidra

POTATOES WITH MUSSEL ESCABECHE & ALIOLI SAUCE

To save time preparing this pintxo, I often use a large can of good-quality mejillones en escabeche (mussels escabeche). This time, I made my own in cider vinegar – it is really easy to do, just remember to do it the day before serving.

First, prepare the mussels. Rinse the mussels thoroughly under cold running water, scrubbing away any barnacles. Remove the beard from each mussel by pulling away the stringy thread from the side of the shell. Tap any mussels that are open. Discard any mussels that remain open or have a broken shell.

Tip the mussels into a large saucepan with a tight-fitting lid. Add the bay leaf. Place the pan over a high heat and cover with the lid. When it starts to steam, cook the mussels for 3–4 minutes, occasionally shaking the pan. The mussels are cooked once the shells have opened. Discard any mussels that remain closed. Leave to cool, then remove the mussels from their shells and place in a bowl. Set aside.

To prepare the escabeche, heat the olive oil in small frying pan/skillet over a low heat. Add the garlic, then once it has taken on a little colour, add the cloves and peppercorns. After a few seconds, stir in the flour. Remove the pan from the heat and immediately stir in both the sweet and hot smoked paprika, followed by the vinegar and wine. Add the thyme and a little salt, to taste. Return the pan to a medium heat and cook, stirring, for a minute or so. If needed, add a splash of water to loosen. Pour the escabeche over the steamed mussels, cover the bowl with cling film/plastic wrap and leave in the fridge overnight. The mussels will be ready to serve the next day.

Fill a large pan with plenty of salted water. Add the potatoes and bring to the boil, then cook until tender. Leave to cool. Once cool enough to handle, peel the potatoes and cut them into thick slices, discarding the ends of the potatoes as you only want the largest thickest ones here.

To assemble the pintxos, top each potato slice with parsley leaves, then a mussel and a blob of alioli. Drizzle over a few spoonfuls of the escabeche juice and a few drops of extra virgin olive oil. Finish with lots of freshly ground black pepper before serving.

4 large waxy potatoes, left unpeeled
handful of flat-leaf parsley, leaves picked
1 quantity of alioli (see page 64)
good-quality Spanish extra virgin olive oil

MUSSELS ESCABECHE
1 kg/2¼ lb. live mussels
1 bay leaf
50 ml/3½ tablespoons Spanish extra virgin olive oil
2 garlic cloves, peeled and sliced
2 whole cloves
6 whole black peppercorns
1 teaspoon plain/all-purpose flour
1 teaspoon sweet smoked paprika
¼ teaspoon hot smoked paprika
100 ml/⅓ cup cider vinegar
50 ml/3½ tablespoons dry white wine
2 fresh thyme sprigs, leaves picked
salt, to taste

MAKES 8–12

Las croquetas de gambas de Daniel
DANIEL'S PRAWN CROQUETTES

Over the last 15 years in Spanish professional kitchens, including many Michelin star establishments, we have seen an increasing interest in recetas de toda la vida (historical recipes), those our grandmothers and even their grandmothers prepared at home. In the hands of creative chefs, these historical recipes – especially croquetas (croquettes) – have gained enthusiasts both at home and abroad.

This recipe has been contributed by my son, Daniel Taylor. It is a celebration of our trips to the Gastronomic Congress in San Sebastián. I use very fine Spanish breadcrumbs for croquetas, however Daniel prefers Japanese panko crumbs, which he blitzes in a blender to make them extra fine. You can make these croquetas well in advance, then keep them in the fridge covered with a cloth ready for frying.

PRAWN STOCK
250 g/9 oz. raw king prawns/jumbo
   shrimp, left in their shells
1 onion, peeled and quartered
2 carrots, peeled and chopped
5 whole black peppercorns

CROQUETAS MIXTURE
75 g/⅓ cup butter (or use light olive oil)
100 g/¾ cup plain/all-purpose flour
1 litre/4 cups full-fat/whole milk,
   warmed
60 ml/¼ cup prawn stock (see above)

TO FINISH
2 eggs
250 g/2½ cups extra fine breadcrumbs
   or Japanese panko breadcrumbs
olive oil, sufficient for deep-frying

large piping/pastry bag

MAKES 20

Peel the prawns, reserving the heads and shells for the stock. Chop the tails into small pieces and set aside.

To make the prawn stock, place the reserved heads and shells in a large saucepan with the onion, carrots and peppercorns. Pour in enough water to cover and place over a medium heat until almost boiling. Skim off any foam that appears on the surface; keep doing this until the stock stays clear. Keeping the heat low, gently simmer the stock, uncovered, for 30 minutes, or until reduced by a third. Strain the stock through a fine-mesh sieve/strainer and set aside.

To make the croquetas mixture, melt the butter in a saucepan over a medium heat. Gradually add the flour, stirring with a wooden spoon to make a paste. Using a whisk, slowly add the warm milk and prawn stock to the paste, whisking continuously until the raw flour taste has gone – this takes 30–40 minutes. Add the reserved prawns, stir well for a couple of minutes and then transfer the mixture to a bowl. Cover the bowl with cling film/plastic wrap and leave to cool completely. Once cool, scrape the mixture into a piping/pastry bag and chill in the fridge for at least 15 minutes. Meanwhile, break the eggs into a shallow bowl and beat them well (this is important). Divide the breadcrumbs between two shallow bowls.

To shape the croquetas, pipe several small logs (each about 35 g/1¼ oz). Grease your hands with oil and then roll the croqueta in the first bowl of breadcrumbs to coat. Next, dip the croqueta in the well beaten egg and, lastly, place the croqueta in the second bowl of breadcrumbs, making sure it is fully coated. Repeat until all the croquette mixture has been used.

Fill a heavy-based saucepan or deep fryer no more than two-thirds full with the oil. Heat to 180°C/350°F. (Use a thermometer to maintain the temperature and avoid the croquetas splitting.) Working in batches, carefully lower the croquetas into the hot oil and cook for 2 minutes, or until crisp and golden. Serve warm.

Bacalao frito con piperrada y pimiento de Gernika
FRIED SALTED COD ON TOAST WITH BASQUE PEPPERS

Basques have a long history of searching the North Atlantic Ocean for their beloved fish, cod. Present in so many Basque dishes, bacalao is cod that is most often dried and salted. Basques hold the secret of converting this unattractive salted fish into something very palatable and quite distinctive, only equalled in la cocina Portuguesa (Portuguese cuisine). While I have included a number of recipes with salted cod in this book, I decided to prepare this dish with fresh cod that I lightly salted myself using a simple method that brings back, in a modern way, some of the attraction of salted cod.

While this pintxo is equally good with padrón peppers on top, on your next visit to the Basque Country, I strongly recommend buying some Gernika peppers, an iconic ingredient of Basque cooking. It is a green pepper, quite small and with a soft skin. It is mostly sweet but with a light lingering peppery touch which is quite addictive. Gernika in Basque, or Guernica in Castilian, is the name of the town devastated by the merciless bombing during the Spanish Civil War. It is also of course the title of one of Picasso's most famous paintings.

The secret to the piperrada (pepper sauce) is to cook all the ingredients slowly so the individual flavours have time to mingle and mellow.

Spanish flour for frying fish is a blend of plain/all-purpose flour and harina de maíz (maize flour). It can be purchased in Spanish specialist shops and on the internet.

SALTED COD
30 g/1 oz. salt
200 g/7 oz. skinless, boneless cod fillet
10 g/¼ oz. plain/all-purpose flour
30 g/1 oz. maize flour
olive oil, sufficient for deep frying

PIPERRADA (PEPPER SAUCE)
3 tablespoons Spanish olive oil
1 onion, peeled and thinly sliced
2 garlic cloves, peeled and sliced
1 green and 1 red (bell) pepper, deseeded and thinly sliced
150 g/5½ oz. tomatoes, skinned, deseeded and finely chopped
1 teaspoon sherry vinegar (optional)

TO FINISH
2 tablespoons Spanish olive oil
4 baguette slices, toasted
4 Gernika or padrón peppers
pinch of coarse sea salt flakes

MAKES 4

First, salt the cod. Dissolve the salt in 1 litre/4 cups water in a large bowl, submerge the cod and leave to soak for 2 hours. Remove the cod, pat dry and set aside.

For the (bell) peppers, heat the oil in a frying pan/skillet. Add the onions and garlic, then gently sauté until translucent. Add the (bell) peppers and sauté until their juices evaporate. Add the tomatoes and vinegar, if using, then cook, stirring, for 10–12 minutes. Set aside.

Slice the cod into four. Combine both flours in a shallow bowl and coat the cod. Heat the oil to 180°C/350°F in a deep frying pan/skillet. Working in batches, carefully lower the cod into the hot oil and cook for a few minutes. Transfer to paper towels and keep warm.

In a separate pan, dry fry the Gernika or padrón peppers until lightly charred. Sprinkle with sea salt.

Top each slice of toast with a spoonful of bell peppers, a piece of fried cod and a Gernika or padrón pepper. Drizzle with a few drops of the liquid from the peppers.

Sardinillas con guacamole en tostada
GUACAMOLE ON TOAST WITH SILVER SARDINES

The Basque Country is a major producer of canned fish, including tuna, anchovies, sardines and sardinillas, which are tiny silver sardines – a true delicacy. Although guacamole is Mexican in origin, since the 1980s, it has been used frequently in the preparation of pintxos. If you cannot find a Serrano pepper, use any other similar variety of green chilli/chile pepper. Do not make the guacamole too far in advance, as it will quickly discolour.

12 baguette slices, toasted
125 g/4 oz. sardinillas (small silver
  sardines) canned in olive oil

GUACAMOLE
2 ripe avocados
100 g/3½ oz. red or white onion,
  peeled and finely chopped
1 small tomato, skinned, deseeded
  and finely chopped
½ Serrano chilli/chile pepper
  (or use jalapeño), deseeded and
  finely chopped
30 g/1 cup coriander/cilantro leaves,
  roughly chopped
juice of ½ lime
salt and freshly ground black pepper

12 cocktail sticks/toothpicks (optional)

MAKES 12

First, make the guacamole. Halve the avocados and remove the large stones/pits. Scoop out the avocado flesh into a mixing bowl and roughly mash with a fork. (Do not make the avocado completely smooth.) Fold in the chopped onion, tomato, chilli/chile and coriander/cilantro. Squeeze in the lime juice and season with plenty of salt and black pepper. Taste and adjust the lime juice, if needed.

Spoon some guacamole onto each slice of toast and place a small silver sardine on top. Drizzle each sardine with a few drops of olive oil from the can. Sprinkle over plenty of freshly ground black pepper. Spear with a cocktail stick/toothpick to secure, if preferred.

Pintxo de tomate, pimiento del Padrón y jamón Ibérico

TOMATOES, PADRÓN PEPPERS & IBÉRICO HAM ON TOAST

This particular pintxo can be scaled up for brunch; simply increase the quantities and serve on thick slices of the best rustic bread you can find.

3 tablespoons Spanish extra virgin
   olive oil
12 cherry tomatoes, halved
few drops of sherry vinegar
6 padrón peppers
6 slices of rustic bread, toasted
1 fat garlic clove, peeled and halved
6 slices of Ibérico ham (with plenty of fat)
pinch of coarse sea salt flakes

SHERRY REDUCTION
1 tablespoon Pedro Ximénez sherry
2 tablespoons sherry vinegar

MAKES 6

To make the sherry reduction, heat the Pedro Ximénez sherry and sherry vinegar in a small saucepan until it has reduced by one-third.

Heat 1 tablespoon of the olive oil in a frying pan/skillet. Once hot, place the tomatoes, cut side down, in the pan so they are not touching each other. Season with a sea salt. Add a few drops of sherry vinegar along with the sherry reduction, then cook until the tomatoes take on a little colour, turning them only once.

At the same time, in a separate pan, cook the padrón peppers in 1 tablespoon of the olive oil for a few minutes until lightly charred. Season with sea salt.

To assemble the pintxos, rub the toast with the cut-side of the garlic clove, then drizzle with a few drops of the olive oil. Top each slice of toast with some ham, a few tomatoes and a padrón pepper. Serve hot, as soon as possible after cooking the tomatoes and peppers.

Pintxo de txistorra, pimiento del piquillo a la brasa y hojitas de lechuga

TXISTORRA SAUSAGE & PIQUILLO PEPPERS ON TOAST WITH SALAD LEAVES

Txistorra is a very long, thin red sausage, perfect for cooking, and very typical of Navarra. It is often used to prepare pintxos. Made from minced/ground pork, or a combination of pork and beef with a 70% fat content, it also includes garlic salt, sweet smoked paprika and herbs. I love to prepare txistorra in the summertime, either grilled/broiled or cooked on the barbecue.

250 g/9 oz. txistorra (red sausage), cut
   into suitable size pieces to fit the toast
8 canned piquillo peppers
handful of salad leaves of your choice
Spanish extra virgin olive oil, for dressing
splash of sherry vinegar
8 baguette slices, toasted
pinch of coarse sea salt flakes

8 cocktail sticks/toothpicks

MAKES 8

Heat a griddle pan over a medium heat. Once hot, cook the sausage for about 3 minutes or until char lines are beginning to appear. (There is no need to add any oil to the pan due to the high fat content of the sausage.)

Halfway through cooking the sausage, add the peppers to the griddle pan. Cook, turning both the sausage and peppers several times, for a further 2–3 minutes or until there are clear char lines.

Meanwhile, dress the rocket leaves with a drizzle of extra virgin olive oil, a splash of sherry vinegar and a pinch of sea salt.

To assemble the pintxos, place a pepper on each slice of toast. Add a few rocket leaves and top with a piece of sausage. Spear with a cocktail stick/toothpick to secure. Serve hot.

Medias noches de jamón y queso
MIDNIGHT BUNS FILLED WITH HAM & CHEESE

Medias noches (midnight buns) are light, slightly sweet, brioche-style buns that are traditionally filled with something salty. The contrasting sweetness and saltiness is key. In our family, these buns are prepared for birthdays and other celebration days. I most often fill them with the traditional ham and cheese, but they are equally delicious with Manchego cheese and membrillo (quince paste). These buns are also fun prepared as mini burgers with all the classic trimmings, speared by a cocktail stick/toothpick. You can buy these buns ready-made, but they are not a patch on ones made at home.

MIDNIGHT BUNS
12 g/½ oz. fresh yeast or 6 g/¼ oz. dried
   yeast
125 ml/½ cup warm full-fat/whole milk
40 g/3¼ tablespoons caster/superfine
   sugar
400 g/3 cups strong white flour, sifted,
   plus extra for dusting
5 g/1 teaspoon salt
2 large/US extra-large eggs
60 g/¼ cup unsalted butter, at room
   temperature
1 egg, beaten, for glazing

HAM & CHEESE FILLING
600 g/1 lb 4 oz. Serrano or York ham
600 g/1 lb 4 oz. Idiazabal or Manchego
   semicurado cheese

*electric stand mixer fitted with dough
   hook attachment*

MAKES 20

Dissolve the yeast in 2 tablespoons of the warm milk with 1 teaspoon of the sugar. Leave it for 4–6 minutes or until it starts to ferment.

Combine the flour, salt, remaining sugar and warm milk in the bowl of an electric stand mixer fitted with the dough hook. Add the bubbling yeast. Start kneading at a low speed to incorporate all the ingredients. Increase the speed slightly before adding the eggs, one by one, and continue kneading. Add the butter and knead again for a further 15 minutes to form a soft, elastic dough.

Using a silicone spatula, scrape the dough onto a work surface lightly dusted with flour. Shape the dough into a ball and transfer to a clean bowl. Cover the bowl with cling film/plastic wrap and leave the dough to rise for about 1 hour or until doubled in volume.

Once risen, turn out the dough onto a work surface lightly dusted with flour. Gently punch the dough to remove some of the air, then re-shape into a ball. Divide the dough into 2 equal pieces. Place one piece in the fridge.

Coat your hands with flour and use more flour on the work surface, if needed. Using the palm of each hand in turn, and barely touching the surface of the dough, roll the dough into a fat sausage. Slice the dough into ten pieces, each about 20 g/¾ oz. Gently punch each portion with your fingers and fold to make small balls. Repeat with the remaining dough from the fridge. Place the dough balls on a baking sheet lined with parchment paper, cover with a clean dish cloth and leave to rise for at least 30 minutes.

Preheat the oven to 180°C/160°C fan/350°F/Gas 4.

Brush the tops of the buns with the beaten egg. Bake in the preheated oven for about 12–15 minutes or until golden, checking them regularly as they can burn easily. Remove from the oven and leave to cool completely. Once cold, slice open each bun with a knife and fill with the ham and cheese, or other filling of your choice.

Gambas con gabardina
PRAWNS DEEP FRIED IN BATTER

The word gabardina means 'rain coat', however in the Spanish kitchen the term refers to coating a piece of food in batter and then deep-frying it. In the Basque Country, many bars serve these battered prawns/shrimp as pintxos. You may find gambas con gabardina in other regions of Spain. I have tasted these prawns in Rioja, in Andalucía and, of course, in my mother's kitchen. She preferred to use carbonated water in her batter rather than beer, as she thought that beer added an unnecessary extra flavour. This is a question of taste. I have enjoyed exceptionally good ones in San Sebastián and in Bilbao, which were deep-fried to perfection.

First, prepare the batter. Using a metal whisk, combine the flour and baking powder in a mixing bowl. Add the saffron and oil, then whisk again. Gradually add the carbonated water or beer while whisking continuously to make a creamy, glossy batter. Add a little more water or beer, if needed. Season with a pinch of salt. Cover the bowl with foil and place in the fridge to rest for at least 30 minutes.

Lightly coat each prawn with a little flour. (The flour helps the batter stick to the prawns.)

Fill a heavy-based saucepan or deep fryer no more than two-thirds full with the oil. Heat to 180°C/350°F. (Use a thermometer to maintain the temperature and avoid the prawns becoming greasy.)

Working in batches, pick up each prawn up by the tail between your finger and thumb, then dip it in the batter. Carefully lower the prawns into the hot oil (use kitchen tongs to do this to protect your fingers from the hot oil) making sure they do not touch each other. In a few seconds, the batter will start to puff up and turn golden. Cook for a minute, turning them only once. Using a slotted spoon, transfer the deep-fried prawns to paper towels to absorb any excess oil. Repeat with the rest of the prawns. Serve hot with mahonesa sauce or your preferred dip.

12 raw king prawns/jumbo shrimp, peeled but with tails left intact
plain/all-purpose flour, for coating
sunflower oil or light Spanish olive oil, for deep-frying
1 quantity of mahonesa sauce (see page 64) or your favourite dip, to serve

BATTER
125 g/1 cup plain/all-purpose flour
1 teaspoon baking power
pinch of saffron, dissolved in a little hot water
1 teaspoon olive oil
100 ml/⅓ cup carbonated water or Spanish beer
pinch of salt

12 cocktail sticks/toothpicks

MAKES 12

Pintxo patatas canallas con chorizo y torreznos de panceta curada

SCOUNDREL POTATOES WITH CHORIZO & PORK CRACKLING

We tend to visualise pintxos as tantalizing morsels of several different ingredients threaded onto a cocktail stick/toothpick. However, now more than ever before, the variation of ingredients and their presentation has become increasingly exciting and unique. As I love patatas canallas (scoundrel potatoes), I decided to make this recipe from Bilbao into a pintxo. Torreznos are small pieces of cured pork belly that have been fried or baked to make crackling (see page 25).

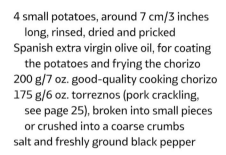

4 small potatoes, around 7 cm/3 inches long, rinsed, dried and pricked
Spanish extra virgin olive oil, for coating the potatoes and frying the chorizo
200 g/7 oz. good-quality cooking chorizo
175 g/6 oz. torreznos (pork crackling, see page 25), broken into small pieces or crushed into a coarse crumbs
salt and freshly ground black pepper

MAKES 8

Preheat the oven to 180°C/160°C fan/350°F/Gas 4.

Using your hands, coat the potatoes in olive oil and then wrap them in foil. Bake in the preheated oven for about 30 minutes, or until tender.

Meanwhile, remove the skin from the chorizo and roughly chop into chunks. Place the chorizo in a food processor or blender and pulse to a coarse paste with a grainy texture.

Heat a little olive oil in a frying pan/skillet and sauté the chorizo until it releases its own oil. Using a slotted spoon, transfer the chorizo meat to a bowl and set aside. Leave the chorizo oil in the pan and set aside.

When the potatoes are baked, remove them from the oven and leave to cool slightly. (But do not turn the oven off as the potatoes are warmed again before serving.) Once cool enough to handle, cut each potato in half lengthways and carefully scoop out some of the centre into the bowl with the chorizo meat. Mix the baked potato and fried chorizo together well.

To assemble the pintxos, re-fill the potato shells with some of the potato and chorizo mixture. Drizzle over a little of the reserved chorizo oil from the pan, then top with the pork crackling pieces or crumbs. Place the filled potatoes on a baking sheet and return to the oven to warm through. Serve hot.

Ensaladilla de siempre
CLASSIC RUSSIAN SALAD

In Spain, ensaladilla Rusa (Russian salad) or just ensaladilla (salad) is a celebration of both the potato and salsa mahonesa (mahonesa sauce). It is a dish served at home, as well as in tapas and pintxos bars. In the Basque Country, this salad is often used in the preparation of a number of pintxos. It is usually made with ingredients such as potatoes, carrots, peas, roasted red (bell) peppers, green olives, hard-boiled eggs, bonito (skipjack tuna) in escabeche or olive oil or cured anchovies. Nowadays creative chefs are using a variety of ingredients, but I have to say that I prefer the ensaladilla de siempre (classic Russian salad) exactly as it has been made in our family for generations, passed from mother to daughter or, in my case, from mother to son. I always make the mahonesa sauce by hand; if you prefer, you can use a handheld stick (immersion) blender. The quantities for the salad given here serve 6 as a starter. If you are using the salad for pintxos or tartaletas, you can easily reduce the amounts.

1 kg/2¼ lb. potatoes, left unpeeled
2 carrots, peeled and chopped into small cubes
150 g/1 cup peas, fresh or frozen
2 large/US extra-large eggs, hard-boiled/cooked, peeled and roughly chopped
200 g/7 oz. bonito (skipjack tuna) canned in escabeche or olive oil, flaked by hand, reserving the oil
6 marinated green olives, stoned/pitted and roughly chopped
2 piquillo peppers, roughly chopped
1 quantity of mahonesa sauce (see page 64)

TO FINISH
1 large/US extra-large egg, hard-boiled/cooked, peeled and grated
1 piquillo pepper, thinly sliced
handful of flat-leaf parsley, finely chopped

SERVES 6

Place the potatoes in a large saucepan filled with plenty of salted water. Bring to the boil over a high heat, then reduce the heat slightly and cook the potatoes until tender. The cooking time will vary depending on the size of the potatoes. Do not overcook the potatoes as they can break apart. Drain and leave to cool. Once cool enough to handle, peel the potatoes and cut them into small cubes roughly the same size as the diced carrots.

Meanwhile, boil the diced carrots in a separate saucepan until tender. Do the same with the peas. Refresh the vegetables under cold running water, then drain and set aside.

In a large mixing bowl, combine the cooked potatoes, carrots and peas with the chopped hard-boiled eggs, flaked bonito (skipjack tuna), chopped green olives, chopped piquillo peppers and a couple of tablespoons of the mahonesa sauce. Stir together to mix well.

Transfer the salad to a serving dish or platter. Spoon over the rest of the mahonesa sauce and garnish with the grated hard-boiled egg, sliced piquillo pepper and chopped parsley.

FROM THE VEGETABLE GARDEN

Vegetable dishes to tempt

Vegetables: A wealth of produce

The Basque Country is shaped by its exciting but tricky geography, the Atlantic weather, the independent spirit of the locals and their passion for fresh seasonal produce and other artisan foods.

By the time I started writing about Basque Spain, modernisation had long been on its way, even though old *caseriós* (traditional farmhouses) in hidden green valleys had been resistant to change. At that time, and up until three or four decades ago, villages, towns and cities were still stocked mostly with produce grown in the vegetable gardens belonging to the women of the *caseriós* in the fertile areas of Navarra. Today, the modern world of growing and supplying food has changed this custom beyond recognition. I have seen how the healthy society of rural women, who bring their excess garden produce to local markets, has been threatened almost to the point of extinction. The year-round availability and low prices offered by modern supermarkets are virtually impossible to match.

I miss the strong local accents of the sellers that would let me know where I was; I miss the familiar faces of those women who tend their precious vegetables gardens and their well-used decorative baskets, all of whom I see less and less. However, hope is returning in the way some modern markets are reviving this old spirit for quality fresh produce. Driven by demand for seasonal fruit and vegetables, which taste just as they used to, from the all-powerful Basque hospitality and catering industry, these new markets are rising out of the ashes of the older ones, even if only a small proportion of what is on sale is grown in the *caseriós*.

Which are the vegetables that are most strongly associated with Basque food today? For me, Basque (bell) peppers, both red and green, fresh, dried or preserved, occupy a prime position. I cannot imagine some of the most renowned dishes cooked with eggs, meat, fish or greens without Basque peppers. Some of these dishes I have included in this book: the *piperrada* or *pipérade*, the celebrated *marmitako* and the stuffed *piquillo* peppers are among many others. Basque peppers have unique names: the fresh or dry red *choriceros*, the green *piparras*, cured or fresh, the Llodosa peppers usually canned, the hot red *guindillas* or the sweet *pimientos del cristal*. The French *piment d'Espelette* also has to be included in the list of Basque peppers.

Basques adore peas and especially the minute ones known as *lagrima* (tear drops), sourced in the spring by top chefs prepared to pay ridiculous prices to prepare amazing dishes adored by all. Quite different from the garden peas we normally cook with, they are tiny, fragile, of a different shape and with an amazing flavour. Salads are often present on the Basque table prepared with the popular *cogollos* which are Little Gem lettuces from Tudela, the *escarola* (frisée or curly endive) and the young cardoons, which are particularly delicious in Navarra.

Leeks, combined with carrots, apples and *cebolletas* (spring onions/scallions), are gently sautéed in olive oil and then passed through a sieve/strainer to make delicious sauces, often served with small game such as quail. The *cebolleta* is one of my favourite ingredients, but unfortunately I find very difficult to find outside of Spain. *Cebolletas* are not young *cebollas* (onions). They belong to a particular species of the genus Allium. They have a milder taste and need to be kept in the fridge.

Large cabbages that decorate traditional vegetable gardens are loved by everyone, especially when served with *alubias negras* (black beans), *morcilla* (black pudding/blood sausage) and *piparras*.

Due to the capricious weather conditions in 'green' Spain, tomatoes grown in the Basque Country can have an unbelievable taste. Today they are served

Clockwise from top left: A maize field in Urrestilla; dried choriceros and fresh piparras peppers; a Basque farmhouse; bunches of cebolletas; Overleaf: A farm near the seaside town of Zumaia.

at restaurants and *pintxo* bars with very little preparation, just a little salt and some tasty, fresh olive oil. At the end of the summer last year, I was surprised by the quality of a plate of tomatoes that had been locally grown and served at La Gambara, one of the most highly regarded bars and restaurants in San Sebastián where people are prepared to wait in long queues for the pleasure.

Southern Navarra has always been a vegetable kingdom, supplier to the Basque Country of peppers, artichokes, cardoons, white asparagus, borage or frisée, Little Gem lettuce and other produce, especially in the spring. I would encourage anyone to taste such local produce in both modern and very traditional Basque restaurants. If I could only find borage, not the flowers but the leaves and stems, which are not particularly well known in other parts of Spain, to enjoy boiled with a few potatoes and drizzled with a fruity olive oil, I would be very happy.

Tomates asados con tomillo
ROASTED TOMATOES WITH THYME

When I first moved to Britain in the 1970s, I quickly realised that I needed to adapt to the British way of eating. Not only do the Brits eat at different times of the day, lots of components of the same meal are served on one plate – a piece of meat or fish with potatoes and vegetables, for example. More than fifty years later, I now do what the British do, except when I cook dishes from my own country, particularly those with a very strong culinary tradition. I follow the way people normally eat when in Spain. I love to serve an entire plate of vegetables, dressed with olive oil and garlic, or these simply roasted, ripe tomatoes with olive oil and thyme.

4–6 ripe tomatoes, preferably on the vine, washed and dried
25 ml/1½ tablespoons Spanish extra virgin olive oil
2–3 garlic cloves, peeled and left whole
sprigs of fresh or dried thyme, to taste
salt and freshly ground black pepper

SERVES 2

Preheat the oven to 180°C/160°C fan/350°F/Gas 4.

Make a few small cuts in the skin of each tomatoes, then place in an ovenproof dish. Drizzle with the olive oil and season with plenty of salt and black pepper. Tuck the garlic cloves and thyme sprigs in the dish amongst the tomatoes.

Roast the tomatoes in the preheated oven for about 25–30 minutes or until soft and juicy. Serve with grilled/broiled meat or fish.

Crema de coliflor
CAULIFLOWER PURÉE

Las cremas de verduras (vegetable purée), which Spanish mothers insist their children must eat, can either be a bit boring or utterly delicious, depending on how it is made. What is needed are a few personal touches, which the cook knows will encourage those same children to continue to cook these recipes as they grow up. La crema de coliflor (cauliflower purée) is one of the most popular vegetable purées made at home.

2 tablespoons Spanish olive oil
1 white onion, peeled and finely chopped
1 leek, white part only, cleaned and chopped
1 large cauliflower, cleaned and cut into medium florets
1 litre/4 cups light vegetable stock or water
100 ml/⅓ cup single/light cream
knob/pat of butter
splash of sherry vinegar or white wine vinegar
salt and freshly ground black pepper
handful of croutons, to serve
chopped chives, to serve

SERVES 4

Heat the olive oil in a saucepan. Add the onion and leek and sauté until they take on a light colour. Add the cauliflower florets and sauté with the leeks and onion for 2–3 minutes, then pour in enough stock or water to cover. Season with a little salt, if needed. Bring to the boil over a high heat, then reduce the heat, add the cream and butter and gently simmer for about 30 minutes or until the cauliflower florets are tender. Remove the pan from the heat, leave to cool slightly, then add the splash of vinegar to taste.

Transfer the cauliflower mixture to a food processor or blender and blitz until light and very creamy. Taste and adjust the seasoning, if needed. Serve with a few croutons and some finely chopped chives.

Guisantes con cebolleta y jamón Serrano

FRESH PEAS WITH SPRING ONIONS & SERRANO HAM

Early spring is the time to visit local markets in the Basque Country. Small baskets of fresh peas, as well as shelled broad beans, are sold there by local farmers. This is the perfect time to enjoy them not as an accompaniment to meat or fish, but as a good portion at the centre of the plate. The cebolleta (Allium fistolosum) should not be confused with the cebolla (Allium cepa). They are two different vegetables, both equally important in Spanish cookery. The cebolleta is milder and can be used raw in salads. Outside of Spain, I suggest using the fat spring onions that are available at this time of year.

Spanish olive oil, for frying
1 onion, peeled and sliced
5 large cebolletas (or use spring onions/
    scallions), white parts only, peeled and
    finely sliced
1 Little Gem lettuce, cut into thin wedges
50 g/1¾ oz. Serrano ham, chopped
2 tablespoons plain/all-purpose flour
750 g/5 cups shelled fresh peas
1 teaspoon sugar
freshly boiled water, as required
salt and freshly ground black pepper

SERVES 4

Heat the olive oil in a large saucepan. Add the onion and very gently sauté for about 10 minutes or until translucent but not coloured. Add the spring onions/scallions and, after a further 10 minutes, add the lettuce and ham. Sprinkle over the flour, stir well and then add the peas and sugar. Slowly add some boiled water, little by little, stirring continuously to dissolve the flour, until the peas are almost covered. Once the peas start to boil, cover the pan with a lid and cook until tender. Serve warm.

Ensalada de escarole rizada, nueces y granada

ESCAROLE LETTUCE, WALNUTS & POMEGRANATE SEEDS

Such a simple recipe and yet so pleasing. Escarole lettuce is sometimes sold in the UK under the French name frisée, but they are not easy to find except during the autumn/fall. A variety of curly endive with pale-green or yellowish leaves and a bushy appearance, escarole has a slightly bitter taste that pairs well with fresh fruit, seeds and nuts. Escarole tend to be on the large side, so I have used only half in this recipe.

½ large escarole lettuce
    (or frisée or curly endive)
seeds of 1 pomegranate
handful of shelled walnuts, halved
    and roughly chopped

DRESSING
40 ml/2½ tablespoons Spanish olive oil
20 ml/4 teaspoons apple cider vinegar
salt and freshly ground black pepper

SERVES 4

Gently rinse the escarole lettuce leaves. Discard any leaves that look tired. Pat dry and place in a large serving dish or on a platter.

Whisk together all the ingredients for the dressing in a small bowl until emulsified. Drizzle the dressing over the escarole lettuce leaves. Scatter over the pomegranate seeds and walnuts just before serving.

Espárragos frescos blancos y trigueros en vinagreta de pimiento rojo asado y aceituna negra

WHITE & GREEN ASPARAGUS WITH ROASTED PEPPERS & BLACK OLIVE VINAIGRETTE

I am proud to have been made a member of the Cofradía del Espárrago Blanco de Navarra, (Confraternity of White Asparagus of Navarra) because my grandmother was a cook from Navarra. In the cofradía, during a festival in April to celebrate their arrival in Corella, I learned how to peel asparagus without breaking the tips. Gathered that morning, the spears were boiled in water with a little salt, sprinkled with a few drops of olive oil and eaten warm – they were perfection. Here, I have used both white and green asparagus dressed with a tasty vinaigrette. It is worth buying black Empeltre olives. I now buy them loose at my local Sunday market in London, but they are available in jars from Spanish specialists.

24 thick white asparagus spears
12 thin green asparagus spears
Spanish olive oil, for frying

VINAIGRETTE
3 tablespoons Spanish extra virgin olive oil
2 tablespoons white wine vinegar
few drops of sherry vinegar
1 small red (bell) pepper, roasted
   (this can be from a jar) and finely diced
6–7 black olives (Empeltre from Navarra,
   if possible)
1 teaspoon mustard seeds,
   toasted in olive oil for a few seconds
salt and freshly ground black pepper

SERVES 4

To prepare the vinaigrette, whisk the olive oil with the vinegars in a jug/pitcher until emulsified. Season with salt and black pepper, then add the diced red (bell) pepper, black olives and toasted mustard seeds. Mix well to combine and set aside.

To prepare the white asparagus, using a sharp knife, trim 1 cm/½ inch from the bottom of each spear. Gently holding each one by the tip as they are brittle, shave off all the thicker layers down the spear with a vegetable peeler. Do not shave any part of the tip. When ready, take 6 spears and tie into a bundle with string, once just below the tips and again near the bottom of the spears.

Bring a large saucepan of salted water to the boil. Drop the bundles of white asparagus into the pan and cook for 15–20 minutes or until tender (the cooking time depends on their thickness). Drain, then once cool enough to handle, remove the strings.

Place both the white and green asparagus spears on a hot griddle pan, drizzle with a little olive oil and cook until both take on some colour. Place on a serving platter, pour over the vinaigrette and season with plenty of black pepper. Serve warm.

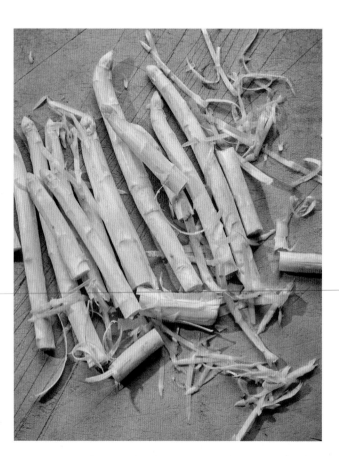

Puerros con sopa de almendras y peras
ALMOND SOUP WITH ROASTED LEEKS & PEAR

A few months ago I tasted an amazing soup prepared by the chef of Gerald's Bar, a restaurant in San Sebastián where vegetarian dishes are brilliantly original and utterly delicious. It was so magical that it inspired me to try a similar combination of ingredients. As I do not have his recipe, I hope the chef approves of my take on the idea. I have made the soup with fresh almonds, but you can use good-quality peeled almonds and tenderise them in boiling water.

Preheat the oven to 180°C/160°C fan/350°F/Gas 4.

To prepare the leeks, remove the roots and trim the green tops. Cut the remaining white parts into 2 or 3 equal pieces. Place the leeks in an ovenproof dish with the garlic. Drizzle over the olive oil and 2 tablespoons cold water. Season with salt and black pepper.

Roast the leeks in the preheated oven for 1 hour, or until tender. Remove the dish from the oven and set aside to cool. Once cool enough to handle, remove and discard the harder, outermost part of the leeks.

To prepare the almond soup, blanch the garlic clove in boiling water for 2 minutes. Place the almonds and blanched garlic in a blender. With the blender running, gradually add the olive oil, little by little, and blitz until smooth. Add the sherry vinegar and 200 ml/¾ cup water, then blend again to a very smooth texture. Set aside.

Just before serving, peel and slice the pear into thin wedges. Ladle the almond soup into deep bowls, then top with the roasted leeks, pear slices and a few fresh or blanched whole almonds. Drizzle with a few drops of olive oil and season with black pepper.

2 small leeks, cleaned
1 garlic clove, peeled
2 tablespoons Spanish extra virgin olive oil
1 crisp eating pear, such as Conference, William or Bosc
salt and freshly ground black pepper

ALMOND SOUP
1 garlic clove, peeled
80 g/generous ½ cup white almonds, peeled, plus extra to serve
60 ml/⅓ cup Spanish extra virgin olive oil, plus extra to serve
¼ teaspoon sherry vinegar

SERVES 2

Fritas de alcachofas con salsa mahonesa o alioli

FRIED ARTICHOKES WITH MAHONESA SAUCE OR ALIOLI

In Spain, we all love patatas fritas (fried potatoes), especially when cooked in olive oil, but recently we have been enjoying other types of fritas, including those made with artichokes. They take a little longer to prepare but the results are very moreish, especially when served with a homemade mahonesa sauce, with or without garlic. Navarra, Tudela is the capital city of the globe artichoke. They are much appreciated by the Basques and particularly by the people of Navarra. Use very fresh, tightly closed globe artichokes, sliced thinly with a sharp knife. I prefer to make the mahonesa sauce using a metal hand whisk, but you can use a handheld stick (immersion) blender, if you prefer.

4 large globe artichokes, washed
1 lemon, cut in half
olive oil, for frying
sea salt

MAHONESA SAUCE (OR ALIOLI)
2 large/US extra-large egg yolks
few drops of lemon juice
125 ml/½ cup sunflower oil
20 ml/4 teaspoons Spanish olive oil
1 garlic clove, peeled and crushed
    (optional)
sea salt and ground white pepper

SERVES 4

Using a hand whisk, beat together the egg yolks and a pinch of salt with a few drops of lemon juice in a deep bowl. Whisk vigorously until everything is well blended. Whisking continuously, slowly pour in the sunflower oil, little by little, followed by the olive oil. This takes some time, so your hand and arm will get tired. Whisk in both directions and change hands frequently. Taste and adjust the seasoning with salt and white pepper, if needed. Whisk in a few drops of warm water and more lemon juice to taste. The emulsion will now be lighter in texture and paler in colour. If making alioli, add the garlic at this point and mix well. Cover the bowl with cling film/plastic wrap and chill in the fridge until required.

Fill a large bowl with plenty of water, add the juice of half a lemon and keep it nearby. Next, prepare the artichokes one by one. Pull off the hard outer leaves until you reach the softer leaves that are lighter in colour. Using a sharp knife, trim the bottom of each artichoke, leaving a small section of the stem. Cut away the top quarter, which is also hard. Artichokes oxidise rapidly, so to prevent them turning grey in colour, rub them lightly all over with the cut side of the other lemon half. Slice the artichokes thinly lengthways from the tip to the bottom of the stem and immediately place them in the bowl of water along with the two lemon halves.

Fill a heavy-based saucepan or deep fryer no more than two-thirds full with the oil. Heat to 180°C/350°F. (Use a thermometer to maintain the temperature throughout cooking.)

When ready to cook, drain the artichokes and pat them dry with paper towels. Working in batches, carefully lower the artichoke slices into the hot oil and cook for 3 minutes, or until crisp and golden. Transfer to paper towels to absorb any excess oil and keep warm while you cook the remaining artichokes.

Sprinkle with a little sea salt, then serve hot with the mahonesa sauce or alioli in a bowl for dipping.

Menestra de primavera de Tudela
SPRING VEGETABLE STEW FROM TUDELA

Tudela is a town in Southern Navarra renowned for the quality of the vegetables grown in the unique rich land that surrounds the town. Tudela is also associated with a dish cooked there all year around, its ingredients changing with the seasons. The dish is known as menestra. To include it in this book, I have chosen a menestra de primavera made with spring vegetables.

Spring is the time of year when hundreds of vegetable gardens, located close to the river Ebro, are uniquely vibrant with a diversity of produce that is needed to prepare a number of dishes admired all over the Basque Country. Menestra de primavera demands a selection of early vegetables, each prepared separately as they require different cooking times. This is a recipe that takes time and an understanding of each vegetable, but it is worth the effort. It is a true ode to the arrival of spring.

Although traditional cooks would cook each vegetable until very tender, too tender perhaps, I prefer to leave the asparagus, broad (fava) beans and fresh peas still with a little bite. You can easily keep this stew vegan by simply omitting the chorizo and ham.

250 g/9 oz. green beans
150 g/5½ oz. shelled broad (fava) beans
6 medium artichoke hearts
150 g/5½ oz. shelled fresh peas
1 bunch of green asparagus
50 ml/3½ tablespoons Spanish extra
   virgin olive oil
½ onion, peeled and finely chopped
20 g/¾ oz. chorizo, thinly sliced
   (optional)
10 g/¼ oz. ham with plenty of fat,
   chopped into cubes and lightly dusted
   with flour (optional)
1 tablespoon plain/all-purpose flour
50 ml/scant ¼ cup dry white wine
salt

SERVES 6

Fill five separate saucepans with salted water and bring to the boil. (This is important as each vegetable has a different cooking time.) Start adding each vegetable to their own pan and cook until tender: first, add the green beans, followed by the broad (fava) beans and artichoke hearts, then the peas and asparagus.

While the vegetables are cooking, prepare the other ingredients. Heat the oil in a frying pan/skillet. When hot, add the onion and sauté until translucent. Add the chorizo and ham, if using, and cook for a few minutes. Sprinkle in the flour and, using a wooden spoon, stir into the other ingredients until well combined and the flour loses its raw flavour. Pour in the wine and let it reduce a little while dissolving the flour. Now, add a splash of the cooking water from the asparagus pan and gently stir to slightly thin the sauce.

Drain each vegetable. Starting with the green beans, layer the vegetables in a large, shallow frying pan/skillet or heatproof dish. Follow with a layer of broad beans, then the artichoke hearts, asparagus and, finally, the peas. Pour the sauce over the vegetables, briefly shake the pan and cook for a further minute before serving.

Cardo rosa con almendras y gambas
PINK CARDOON WITH ALMONDS & PRAWNS

When my grandmother was alive, our family's kitchen had a strong sabor Navarro (Navarran flavour). This is because some of the vegetables she loved were difficult to find away from southern Navarra and Rioja, in particular the cardoon. The cardoon (Cynara cardunculus) is first cousin to the artichoke, borage and endive. It looks like celery, but is much bigger, slightly whiter and the outer strings are tougher, so they need to be removed. When cooked, it becomes tender and very delicate. As well as fresh, you can find frozen or jarred cardoons already prepared. Outside Spain, cardoons can be bought from specialist importers or online.

Just a few years ago in Rioja, I first tasted pink cardoons prepared by Francis Paniego, chef of the restaurant El Echaurren in Ezcaray. He was collaborating with a number of producers to save foods that were under threat, and the pink cardoon was one of them. For me, this is an evocative and truly delicious recipe, well worth the time needed to prepare it.

1 tablespoon plain/all-purpose flour
1 large pink cardoon
4 tablespoons Spanish extra virgin
 olive oil, plus extra as needed
200 g/7 oz. raw large prawns/jumbo
 shrimp, peeled
½ large onion, peeled and finely chopped
1 small dried cayenne pepper, left whole
12 whole almonds, peeled
2 garlic cloves, peeled
1 tablespoon chopped flat-leaf parsley
10 g/¼ oz. toasted flaked/slivered
 almonds
salt and freshly ground black pepper

SERVES 4

Fill a bowl with water, add the flour and stir to dissolve. To prepare the cardoon, remove and discard the hard outer leaves, then wash the rest under cold running water. Using a sharp knife, remove the strings from the outer edges of each leaf. With a damp cloth or brush, clean both sides. Remove the strings from the inner and outer sides by cutting the top with a knife and pulling the strings downwards. Cut each leaf into 5-cm/2-inch strips. Put the cardoon in the bowl of water, leave to soak for 15 minutes, then drain.

Bring a large saucepan of salted water to the boil. Add the soaked cardoon and cook for 30 minutes, or until tender. Remove the pan from the heat and leave the cardoon in the water while you prepare the sauce.

Heat the olive oil in a frying pan/skillet. Add the prawns/shrimp and sauté until they just star to turn pink. Transfer to a plate and set aside.

In the same pan, using the remaining oil very gently sauté the onion for about 15–20 minutes or until translucent but not taking on any colour. Add the cayenne pepper.

In a separate frying pan, sauté the almonds and garlic in a little oil until lightly coloured, then stir in the parsley. Transfer to a mortar, then pound with a pestle until all the ingredients are well blended. Set aside.

Drain the cardoon, reserving the cooking water. Add the cardoon to the pan with the onion. Stir in the almond, garlic and parsley mixture. Shake the pan before adding 150 ml/⅔ cup of the reserved cardoon cooking water and heat through for a few minutes. Return the prawns to the pan to finish cooking. Spoon the cardoon and onions into bowls, then divide the prawns between them. Scatter some almonds on top before serving.

NOTES

» *Red cardoons take less time to cook than white ones.*

» *You can swap the prawns for Serrano or Ibérico ham.*

Porrusalda con patata, puerro y caldo de pollo y ternera
POTATO, LEEK & CARROT STEW COOKED IN A BEEF & CHICKEN STOCK

Porrusalda is a gentle stew with a lovely taste. As with other traditional Basque recipes, there are as many porrusaldas as there are cooks. Some are vegetarian while others may contain bacalao (salt cod), but here I have included one prepared with a tasty, light beef and chicken stock.

Potatoes are fundamental in classic Basque stews. The way they are prepared is still considered by cooks as essential. Cascar is the old way to cut potatoes, just as our mothers and grandmothers used to do: peel the potato and, using a sharp knife, make a small cut and then break off a piece of potato. Once you have cut the first one, repeat for all the rest. Try to cut all the vegetables for into similar-sized pieces.

First, prepare the stock. Heat the oil in a large saucepan. Add the beef and sauté until browned all over. Add the onion and cook, stirring with a wooden spoon, for a few minutes. Add the chicken, cook for a further 5 minutes, then add all the remaining ingredients. Pour in 2 litres/quarts water to cover. Bring to the boil, skimming off any foam that appears on the surface until clear. Reduce the heat and simmer for about 1½ hours. Taste and adjust the seasoning with salt, if needed. Strain the stock (reserving the meat to use later in another dish, see note below) and leave to cool. Place in the fridge for a couple of hours, then remove any solidified fat sitting on the surface of the stock. Set aside until required.

When ready to make the stew, heat 2 tablespoons of the oil in a large saucepan with a lid. Add the leeks and gently sauté for a few minutes, then pour in about 300 ml/1¼ cups water to cover, place the lid on the pan and cook until tender. Add the potatoes, carrot and 400 ml/1⅔ cups of the reserved stock, bring to the boil and cook over a medium heat for about 25–30 minutes or until the potatoes and carrots are tender.

In a separate pan, gently sauté the onion in the remaining olive oil until soft but without taking on any colour. Halfway through cooking the onion, add the garlic. Tip this onion and garlic mixture into the pan with the vegetable stew. Cook, stirring, for a further few minutes before serving.

3 tablespoons Spanish extra virgin olive oil
400 g/14 oz. medium leeks, cleaned and cut into thick slices
400 g/14 oz. medium potatoes, peeled and cut into small chunks (see recipe introduction)
1 carrot, peeled and cut into thick slices
400 ml/1⅔ cups beef and chicken stock (see below)
1 white onion, peeled and finely chopped
2 garlic cloves, peeled and finely chopped
salt, to taste

BEEF & CHICKEN STOCK
2 tablespoons Spanish extra virgin olive oil
250 g/9 oz. stewing beef, chopped into chunks
1 onion, peeled and quartered
250 g/9 oz. skinless chicken, chopped into chunks
1 carrot, peeled and cut into chunks
1 leek (white part with only some of the green part), cleaned and chopped
50 g/⅓ cup dried chickpeas/garbanzo beans, soaked overnight
salt, to taste

SERVES 4

NOTES
» *When straining the stock, reserve the leftover beef and chicken chunks and use them to make some meat and egg croquetas (see page 29).*

» *Sometimes I add a little fresh cream to the finished stew before serving.*

Pimientos del Piquillo rellenos de pescado
PIQUILLO PEPPERS STUFFED WITH WHITE FISH

I don't recall eating canned pimientos del piquillo (piquillo peppers) until I was in my late teens. At that time, I was living in Madrid while their area of production was located in southern Navarra. Piquillos can be purchased fresh, but these small, vivid red, conical peppers with a distinctive flavour become a true speciality once canned or jarred. A couple of decades ago, canned piquillos inspired top Basque chefs to create recipes that were copied everywhere.

Staying once in the small medieval town of Puente la Reina, near Pamplona, I was invited to a seasonal food experience. An industrial roasting oven was set up to char thousands of peppers grown by locals in their gardens. It was impressive to hear the fire crackling as the peppers passed through on a conveyor belt, their skins charring in a matter of minutes. Collected in buckets, the peppers were then taken back to family kitchens to be peeled by hand before being preserved.

Heat half the oil in a large saucepan. Add the onion, garlic, carrot and green (bell) pepper and gently sauté. When all the vegetables are tender, add the flaked white fish and parsley. Season with salt and black pepper. Cook for a few minutes, stirring, then set aside.

Heat the remaining oil in a frying pan/skillet (adding a little extra, if needed). Using a tablespoon, stuff the canned or jarred piquillo peppers with the vegetable and fish mixture, then lightly coat each one in flour. Next, dip each pepper in the beaten egg, add to the pan and fry for a few minutes, turning just once, to take on a little colour. Once fried, transfer to a shallow saucepan or earthenware pot, making sure the peppers are not touching. Keep warm.

Meanwhile, prepare the sauce. Warm the stock. In a small saucepan, gently sauté the onion in the olive oil until tender. Add the red (bell) and piquillo peppers, stirring for a minute before adding the warmed stock and chopped parsley. Simmer for another couple of minutes and then blend using a handheld stick (immersion) blender.

Pour the sauce over the stuffed peppers in the shallow saucepan or earthenware dish. Gently heat for a few minutes before serving.

100 ml/scant ½ cup Spanish extra virgin olive oil, plus extra for frying
1 onion, peeled and finely diced
1 garlic clove, peeled and finely diced
1 carrot, peeled and diced
1 green (bell) pepper, deseeded and diced
200 g/7 oz. fish with firm white flesh (such as hake, cod or monkfish), skinned, boned and flaked
1 tablespoon finely chopped flat-leaf parsley
280 g/10 oz. whole pimientos del piquillo (piquillo peppers), canned or jarred
flour, for coating
2 medium/US large eggs, beaten
salt and freshly ground black pepper

SAUCE
250 ml/1 cup fish stock (see page 10)
½ small onion, peeled and thinly sliced
2–3 tablespoons Spanish olive oil
2 red (bell) peppers, roasted, peeled and deseeded and sliced
2 piquillo peppers, thinly sliced
1 teaspoon chopped flat-leaf parsley
salt, to taste

SERVES 4

Salsa de tomate casera
TOMATO SAUCE

This is a simple, all-round tomato sauce that will keep well in the fridge for up to four days. I prefer to make it with fresh tomatoes when they are in season and perfectly ripe.

100 ml/scant ½ cup Spanish extra virgin olive oil
1 garlic clove, peeled and thinly sliced
½ small onion, peeled and finely chopped (optional)
350 g/12½ oz. fresh or canned tomatoes, puréed
pinch of sugar
salt and freshly ground black pepper

MAKES ABOUT 250 G/9 OZ.

Place a saucepan over a high heat. Add the olive oil and garlic, then fry for just a few seconds. Add the onion, if using, then reduce the heat and sauté for 5 minutes, stirring frequently. Add the tomatoes and simmer until they break down into a sauce, which then reduces by one-third. Season with salt and pepper, then add the sugar.

Pass the sauce through a fine mesh sieve/strainer. The sauce is now ready to use.

This sauce will keep for up to 4 days when covered with a layer of olive oil to keep out the air and stored in the fridge. (I prefer not to freeze this sauce.)

Sakari una salsa Vasco francesa
SAKARI SAUCE

Sakari is a popular French Basque sauce, which can be moderately hot or fairly hot, used mostly to marinate and accompany grilled meats and even fish. I have found different bottled sakari sauces available to purchase, some of them with a long list of ingredients and perhaps not all to the taste of the traditional Basque cook. For this reason, I am including a simple and tasty sakari sauce recipe here, which is easy to prepare at home. It is a lovely sauce to use during the summer when the barbecues are working almost full time in the garden.

50 ml/3½ tablespoons light olive oil or sunflower oil
100 ml/scant ½ cup white wine vinegar
4 garlic cloves, peeled and chopped
2 teaspoons piment d'Espelette (espelette pepper)
pinch of fresh or dried thyme
1 bay leaf
4 flat-leaf parsley sprigs, roughly chopped
salt and freshly ground black pepper

glass preserving bottle with a swing-top stopper

SERVES 8 (DEPENDING ON USE)

Pour the oil and vinegar into the glass preserving bottle. Add the rest of the ingredients to the bottle and seal with the stopper. Place the bottle in a cool, dark place and leave to rest for 5 days, shaking the bottle 3 times each day. On the fifth day, transfer the bottle to the fridge for a further 2 days.

As the oil solidifies in the bottle, take it out of the fridge well in advance of using and allow it to return to room temperature.

AT THE MARKETPLACE

Enjoying mushrooms, eggs & beans

Life in the market

When I was growing up in Spain in the 1950s, refrigeration in many kitchens was dependent on the blocks of ice delivered every day to houses in cities and towns by *el hombre del hielo* (the ice man), who knocked on doors early every morning. Of course, the situation was different in the countryside. Living with insufficient refrigeration for preserving food was one of the reasons why women had to go to the local covered market every day, Monday to Saturday. I believe that going to the market was not necessarily an imposition for most women. Living in the Basque Country, it was the place where women would meet friends and have a cup of coffee with a *pastel de arroz* (rice cake). In rural areas, where farmhouses tended to be dotted at a fair distance from each other, self-sufficiency also meant isolation, which in the case of women could be relieved by selling fresh produce directly to the public at a local market and making some extra cash.

By the end of the 1960s, things had greatly improved both in towns and also in the countryside, mainly due to the introduction in Spain of modern systems of domestic refrigeration and food distribution. By then, women started to find work outside the home. As a result, daily covered markets were visited at all different times of the day, although their future was beginning to look less secure even if the almost total dominance of supermarkets was still in the imagination of many investors.

As time progressed, supermarkets altered how most people bought their food. Following years of decline for covered markets, the opening of spectacular food halls inside the old market buildings has meant the salvation for many of these historical buildings and some revival of market life. Forced by modern ways of living and shopping, some popular weekend street markets have evolved by selling not only fresh produce but also clothing and by serving local food specialities.

What have never be under threat in the Basque Country are a number of historical traditional markets opening a certain day of the week or every day. This is the case of the stunning El Mercado de la Ribera in the city of Bilbao. From early morning and throughout the day, customers can combine their morning shopping routine with a moment or two of food pleasure. In addition to the many attractively displayed food stalls selling all kinds of ingredients, shoppers are surrounded by numerous restaurants and bars, overlooking the river. There is even a cookery school. El Mercado de Abastos in the city of Victoria, in Alava is another great example of the evolution and success of many traditional markets.

When in Guipúzcoa, I strongly recommend a visit to the market of Tolosa to buy some beans, and especially the unique market of Ordicia not far from San Sebastián, dating back to the thirteenth century. Its reputation today is higher than ever. Ordicia is a meeting place for chefs, locals and even tourists. It is held on Wednesdays all through the year. As is often the case, the market takes place in the centre of the town, in the magnificent main square. It was in Ordicia where I became fully aware how important the quality of food was for Basque people, the relevance of the seasons, as well as the kind of ingredients they love to cook with, many still brought to the market by artisan producers from *caseriós*. I saw quality beans, especially black beans, large breads made with wheat or maize flour wrapped in maple leaves, local honey, meat and charcuterie, vegetables and, of course, cheeses.

Many Basque cheeses are still being made by shepherds who graze their sheep in the surrounding valleys and mountains, in southern Guipúzcoa, Alava and Navarra. Some of the best known are Roncal from

the valleys of north eastern Navarra and Idiazábal from Aitzgorry and the Sierra de Aralar, but there are others equally good. You can find the best meat in the region, including *morcilla* (black pudding/ blood sausage), a whole variety of peppers, apples and potatoes to make the perfect stew.

Ordicia is an ideal place to socialise. It opens early, at a time when many customers are having breakfast in the bars and restaurants located in the main square or nearby streets. All day long the polished wooden counters are full of temptation, offering *pintxos* and other specialities of the house made on demand. In spring and autumn/fall, baskets of wild mushrooms known as *zizak* tempt buyers in the market as well as customers in the bars. Basques adore a *tortilla* (omelette) made with the small

perretxicos, a *revuelto* (scrambled eggs) with large ceps or a collection of *zizak*, beautifully marinated. The *perretxico* (*Calocybe gambosa*) is a creamy mushroom also known as *seta de San Jorge* (St. George's mushroom). It is highly aromatic and especially delicious during the spring. It is a great excuse to visit the area.

Clockwise from top left: The facade of El Mercado de la Ribera, Bilbao; baked goods for sale; Idiazábal cheese at the Ordicia farmers' market; a vegetable stall at Tolosa market. Overleaf: The Oria river, Tolosa.

Piperrada Vasca
BASQUE PEPPER STEW

Piperrada in the Spanish Basque provinces and pipérade in the French are sister recipes that demonstrate some slight differences in their preparation and ingredients. There are many versions of this simple, yet great-tasting recipe. French pipérade contains espelette chillies/chiles, while the Spanish piperrada does not. Either way, for the dish to be at its best, it needs good-quality ingredients – the ripest tomatoes and the freshest bell peppers that are in season. It is really a celebration of the pepper and, with that, of summer.

Here, I have followed a recipe for piperrada that is included in a unique book, Alimentos y Guisos en la Cocina Vasca (Basque Cooking and Ingredients), by the late José María Busca Isusi, published in 1983. He insisted that Spanish Basque piperrada 'should not contain red peppers' and so I have included only green peppers. Whether it does or doesn't, piperrada and pipérade are often prepared with meat and fish, although personally I still prefer the original version with eggs.

2 tablespoons Spanish extra virgin olive oil
1 onion, peeled and sliced
2 green (bell) peppers, deseeded and thinly sliced
2 garlic cloves, peeled and chopped
10 g/¼ oz. Serrano ham fat, chopped into small cubes
150 g/5½ oz. tomatoes, peeled and roughly chopped
½ teaspoon dried oregano
2 large/US extra-large eggs, beaten
2 slices of Serrano ham
salt, to taste
handful of flat-leaf parsley, chopped, to garnish
slices of bread, toasted, to serve

SERVES 4

Heat the olive oil in a large, deep frying pan/skillet. Add the onions and sauté until soft. Add the green (bell) peppers and garlic, sprinkle with a little salt and continue cooking, allowing the vegetable juices to slightly evaporate.

Meanwhile, in a separate pan, fry the cubes of Serrano ham fat until they release some of their fat. Add the tomatoes and oregano, then slowly cook for about 10–15 minutes, or until the tomatoes start to break down and release their juices.

Tip the tomatoes into the pan with the onion, pepper and garlic mixture, then cook, stirring, for 1 minute. Add the beaten eggs and cook over a low heat, gently stirring to bring the layer of ingredients at the bottom of the pan to the top. As the eggs will continue cooking in the residual heat, remove the pan from the heat and stir everything once more.

Immediately before serving, gently fry the slices of Serrano ham in a frying pan until they take on a little colour. Garnish the stew with the chopped parsley, then serve with the fried ham slices on top and some toasted bread on the side.

Hongos con vinagreta y hierbas frescas
CEPS WITH A VINAIGRETTE & FRESH HERBS

Thanks to its geography and climate, the Basque Country is a veritable fungi paradise. I recommend a visit to the market of Ordicia, a town situated 34 km/21 miles south of San Sebastián. It is the most outstanding place to find a perfect Caesar's mushroom (Amanita caesarea) or one of the most adored of all mushrooms by the Basques, the cep (Boletus edulis).

200 g/7 oz. fresh ceps
1 tablespoon finely chopped
   flat-leaf parsley
2 tablespoons finely chopped chives
50 g/1¾ oz. Manchego semicurado,
   cut into thin slivers
slices of bread, toasted, to serve

VINAIGRETTE
4–5 tablespoons Spanish extra virgin
   olive oil
1 tablespoon sherry vinegar
salt and freshly ground black pepper

SERVES 4

First, prepare the mushrooms. Using a soft cloth or brush, clean the mushrooms to remove any soil. Do not use water as they will loose their texture and especially their aroma.

Trim the base from the stalk and discard. Using a mandolin or very sharp knife, thinly slice each cep lengthways. Arrange the ceps in a serving dish or platter and then scatter over the chopped herbs.

Combine all the ingredients for the vinaigrette in a small bowl or jar until well mixed. Drizzle the vinaigrette over the ceps, then add the slivers of Manchego. Serve with some toasted bread.

NOTE
» *Large oyster mushrooms are a good substitute for fresh ceps, if needed.*

Revuelto de perretxicos
SCRAMBLED EGGS WITH ST. GEORGE'S MUSHROOMS

Mycology (the study of fungi) is a passion in the Basque Country, particularly during early spring and autumn/fall. Amateurs search the hillsides and woods for prized mushrooms, especially the zizak (group Tricholoma) and boletus, which they use in many dishes.

Whenever I am in the Basque Country in spring, I ask for a plate of perretxicos (Calcybe gambosa). They say that the very best ones are found in the province of Alava. For my money, the smaller the mushrooms, the better. I prefer them prepared in the simplest way possible, which is pan-fried with little else added or cooked in the classic revuelto de perretxicos.

400 g/14 oz. fresh perretxicos
   (St. George's mushrooms), cleaned
3 tablespoons Spanish olive oil
1 onion, peeled and finely chopped
1 garlic clove, peeled and finely chopped
8 medium/US large eggs, beaten
salt and freshly ground black pepper
handful of flat-leaf parsley, roughly
   chopped, to garnish
slices of bread, toasted, to serve

SERVES 4

First, prepare the mushrooms. Using a soft cloth or brush, clean the mushrooms to remove any soil. Do not use water as they will loose their texture and especially their aroma. If they are small, use them whole. If they are large, slice them in half.

Heat the olive oil in a frying pan/skillet. Add the onion and garlic and sauté until soft and taking on a little colour. Reduce the heat, add the mushrooms, cover he pan and gently cook for a few minutes. Season with salt. Pour the beaten eggs into the pan and gently stir to lightly scramble. Do not overcook the eggs. Scatter over the parsley and serve with some toasted bread.

Tortilla de patatas, cebolla morada y pimiento rojo

POTATO OMELETTE WITH CARAMELISED RED ONION & RED PEPPER

Imagine the long counter of a bar situated on the upper floor of the main market in a Basque city. It is loaded with pintxos, including as many different tortillas de patata (potato omelettes) as you can imagine, each one cooked with potatoes, of course, as well as other ingredients: potato and chorizo; potato and (bell) peppers; potato and piquillo peppers; or simply the classic tortilla with potato and caramelised onions. This is exactly what diners will find at El Mercado de la Ribera in Bilbao. I was there a few months ago. It was early morning, but the place was already heaving, full of lively people eating pintxos de tortilla de patata with a large coffee, or even a cold beer.

There is no traditional way of cutting the potatoes when cooking a tortilla. You can slice them thinly, as I do, slice them thickly or even dice them. The potatoes should never be parboiled, but rather gently braised in plenty of olive oil along with, in this case, the onion and red (bell) pepper. The final result is not at all greasy as most of the oil is drained off before the beaten egg is added. As the olive oil remains clean and very flavoursome, it can be reserved and used once more for another dish.

350 ml/1½ cups Spanish olive oil
1 large red onion, peeled and
    thinly sliced
1 large red (bell) pepper, deseeded
    and sliced
1 kg/2¼ lb. potatoes (any slightly
    floury variety, such as Désirée or
    Maris Piper), peeled and thinly sliced
6 medium/US large eggs
salt, to taste

SERVES 6–8

Heat 3 tablespoons of the olive oil in a small frying pan/skillet. Add the onion and gently sauté until soft but not coloured. Halfway through cooking the onion, add the red (bell) pepper and continue cooking, stirring, until both the onion and pepper are equally soft. Set aside.

Select a frying pan/skillet that is light enough to lift with one hand. (I use a non-stick 25-cm/10-inch pan.) Now, select a plate that is large enough to cover the frying pan and light enough to hold with the other hand, when turning the tortilla over. Keep the plate nearby.

Rinse the potato slices, pat dry and season with salt. Gently heat the remaining olive oil in the selected frying pan over a medium heat – to test the oil is hot enough, drop a slice of potato into the pan; if it sizzles, the oil is ready. Slide the potato slices into the hot oil. To make sure the potato does not brown too fast, gently turn them while they cook. When the potatoes are nearly ready, add the sautéed onion and pepper. Once everything is well mixed and the oil comes to the surface, tip it into a colander set over a bowl to drain.

Beat the eggs in a large bowl. Transfer the potatoes, onion and pepper from the colander to the bowl, mixing thoroughly with a fork. Add some salt, if needed.

Pour 1–2 tablespoons of the reserved olive oil into the frying pan to thinly cover the base. When hot, pour the egg mixture into the pan and cook for 2–3 minutes on one side. Using a spatula, lift the tortilla away from one side of the pan to check it is light brown in colour.

Hold the frying pan over the sink. Place the plate on top of the pan, holding it in place with your other hand. Swiftly invert the pan and plate together so the tortilla lands on the plate. Lift off the pan, turn it the right way up, then slide the tortilla back into the pan. Cook on the other side for a further 2–3 minutes. Using a wooden skewer, check the centre of the tortilla which should be set but remain moist. Place a clean plate on top of the pan, then turn out the tortilla. Serve warm or cold.

Tortilla de bacalao, cebolla y pimiento verde

SALT COD OMELETTE WITH ONION & GREEN PEPPER

Together with other specialities, such as bacalao frito (fried salt cod), this dish is part of the food culture of the many sidreras (cider houses) dotted all over the Basque Country.

For a perfect tortilla de bacalao (salt cod omelette), the cod must be first desalted to your personal taste. To desalt the cod, rinse it under cold running water. Place the fillets in a deep saucepan and cover with plenty of fresh water with the skin side facing up. As they are generous pieces, change the water every six hours, two or three times or more, if needed. Before cooking, remove the salt cod fillets from the water, rinse again under the tap and pat dry with paper towels.

When preparing this tortilla, it is important that the onion and green (bell) pepper caramelise by gently sautéing them in olive oil until very tender. I usually make two tortillas, which I divide between four people, and serve them for brunch, on top of toasted slices of bread with a lettuce and tomato salad.

4 large bacalao (salt cod) fillets,
   skin left on and desalted
   (see recipe introduction)
Spanish olive oil, as needed
1 large onion, peeled and thinly sliced
1 green (bell) pepper, deseeded and
   thinly sliced
4 large/US extra-large eggs
salt and freshly ground black pepper
slices of bread, toasted, to serve

SERVES 4

Once the salt cod has been desalted and dried, poach the fillets in plenty of olive oil at 70°C/158°F for 1 hour. (This process is known as templar el bacalao.) Remove the salt cod from the oil. When cool enough to handle, flake the fish.

Meanwhile, sauté the onion and pepper in a few tablespoons of olive oil, stirring often, until very tender and taken on some colour.

Beat the eggs in a large bowl. Add the sautéed vegetables and flaked salt cod, then stir to mix well.

Heat 2 tablespoons of olive oil in a large frying pan/skillet. Add half the egg mixture to the pan and cook for 1 minute before folding into an omelette. Do not overcook the egg.

Repeat with the remaining egg mixture, adding a little more oil, if needed. Serve warm.

Huevos en cazuela

EGGS WITH CHORIZO, HAM, PEPPER, ASPARAGUS & PEAS

Also known as al plato, this is a Basque version of a dish that is prepared in many parts of Spain. A very simple, highly versatile dish that makes the perfect brunch.

150 g/5 oz. tomato sauce (see below)
4 large/US extra-large eggs
2 tablespoons Spanish extra virgin
   olive oil
25 g/1 oz. chorizo, sliced
25 g/1 oz. Serrano ham, chopped
4 green asparagus spears, lightly boiled
75 g/½ cup peas (fresh or frozen),
   lightly boiled
1 roasted red (bell) pepper
   (canned or jarred), sliced
salt, to taste
slices of bread, to serve

TOMATO SAUCE
1 x 400-g/14-oz. can cherry tomatoes
3 garlic cloves, peeled and finely
   chopped
2 tablespoons Spanish olive oil
pinch of salt
pinch of sugar

SERVES 4

First, make the tomato sauce. Tip the canned cherry tomatoes into a food processor or blender, then blitz until smooth. Strain through a fine-mesh sieve/strainer to remove any skins or seeds.

Heat the olive oil in a saucepan. Add the garlic and sauté until it takes on a little colour. Pour the blitzed tomatoes into the pan, then stir in the salt and sugar. Bring to the boil, then reduce the heat, cover and very gently cook for about 1 hour, stirring occasionally. Set aside to cool.

Generously coat a frying pan/skillet with olive oil. If you have one, a traditional Basque cazuela (earthenware pot) is even better. Cover the base of the pan or pot with half of the tomato sauce. Make four wells in the sauce, then carefully crack an egg into each one. Take care not to break the yolks. Season with some salt.

Pour the remaining tomato sauce into the pan or pot around the eggs. Arrange the rest of the ingredients around the pan so that they are all visible. Cook over a medium heat until the egg whites have set but the egg yolks are still runny. Serve with slices of good bread.

Pan de boniato, calabacín y maíz amarillo
SWEET POTATO & COURGETTE CORN BREAD

It is well known that Basques (who were experienced sea farers) were among the early Spanish who travelled and settled in the Americas in the late fifteenth century. Facing the difficulty of maintaining their Spanish diet, they had to adapt to indigenous food, including bread made with corn. While they did not much appreciate the potato, they soon became accustomed to the sweet potato, which they called boniato or batata. With some imagination, they found the sweetness of the boniato reminiscent of pork fat.

Back in northern Spain, due to climatic conditions, wheat was difficult to grow and so corn became part of the staple diet. Corn is used make talos (flatbreads) and, of course, pan de maíz (corn bread). Despite having almost disappeared in the last decades, corn bread has become fashionable again. This recipe can also be made with pumpkin.

250 g/9 oz. sweet potato, peeled and sliced into rounds
250 g/9 oz. courgettes/zucchini, partly peeled with a little skin left on
350 ml/1½ cups full-fat/whole milk
1 tablespoon salted butter
30 g/2 tablespoons granulated white sugar
1 teaspoon cornflour/cornstarch, dissolved in water to make a paste
2 tablespoons double/heavy cream
200 g/7 oz. yellow maize flour (precooked)
3 large/US extra-large eggs, separated, plus an extra egg, for glazing

25 x 15 x 6-cm/9 x 6 x 5½-inch baking tin/pan, greased with butter and dusted with a thin layer of flour

MAKES 1-KG/2¼-LB. LOAF

Preheat the oven to 180°C/160°C fan/350°F/Gas 4.

Place the sweet potato in a saucepan, cover with boiling water and bring back to the boil. Reduce the heat and cook for 5 minutes. Add the courgettes/zucchini and continue to cook until both the sweet potato and courgettes are tender. Drain in a fine-mesh sieve/strainer, reserving 80 ml/⅓ cup of the cooking water. Using a silicone spatula, press out as much moisture from the vegetables in the sieve as possible, then transfer the thick sweet potato purée to a clean muslin/cheesecloth and wring out any excess moisture. Transfer the sweet potato purée to a bowl and set aside.

Put the milk, butter, sugar and cornflour/cornstarch in a large saucepan. Gently warm while stirring to combine. When the butter has melted, remove the pan from the heat. Stir in the sweet potato purée, cream and reserved cooking water. Slowly add the maize flour, then add the egg yolks, one by one, mixing well.

In a separate bowl, beat the egg whites to soft peaks and gently fold into the sweet potato mixture. Scrape this mixture into the prepared baking tin/pan and lightly brush the top with the beaten egg.

Bake the corn bread in the preheated oven for 1 hour, or possibly less. It is best eaten warm. It will keep for up to 4 days when stored in an airtight container, and can be reheated to serve.

Pochas con codornices
WHITE BEANS WITH QUAILS

Basques love beans. They love red beans, black beans and, to a lesser extent, white beans. There is, however, one exception. They adore the type of white haricot bean known as pocha – the name refers to the pale colour of its skin. Pochas are planted at the beginning of summer and, depending on their variety, they are harvested from late August through to the end of October. They are taken out of their pods while still tender, before they become dry. When cooked, their characteristic texture is buttery and delicious. If you cannot find pochas, use any other type of dried white bean from the most recent season and soak them overnight. Pochas do not require soaking.

Combine all the ingredients for the marinade in a large bowl with 150 ml/⅔ cup water. Add the quails to the bowl and submerge in the marinade until well coated. Leave to marinate for at least 1 hour.

Put the beans in a large saucepan and pour in enough water to cover. Add a little salt. Bring to the boil, immediately reduce the heat and simmer for 45 minutes or until tender (dried beans take longer). Add more water as needed. Shake the pan instead of stirring to avoid breaking the beans as they become fragile during cooking.

Meanwhile, prepare the sauce. Heat the olive oil in a saucepan. When hot, add the onion and cook until translucent. Add the garlic, carrot, green and red (bell) peppers. When all the ingredients are tender, add the tomato sauce, stir and cook until some bubbles of oil appear on the surface. Season with salt, then set aside.

Remove the quails from the marinade and pat dry with paper towels. Season with plenty of salt and black pepper. Heat 2–3 tablespoons olive oil in a frying pan/skillet and sauté the quails until they take on a little colour. Transfer them to the pan with the sauce. Stir to combine all the flavours and cook for a further few minutes.

Gently spoon the beans and their cooking liquid to the pan with the quails and sauce. Shake the pan to mix everything together. Cook for about 12 minutes, or until the quails are cooked through. Divide the beans and quails between two individual bowls, then scatter over the chopped chives before serving.

2 quails, cleaned, dressed and cut in half down the breastbone
500 g/1 lb. 2 oz. fresh pochas beans (or use any other dried white beans, soaked overnight)
2–3 tablespoons Spanish extra virgin olive oil, for frying the quails
1 teaspoon finely chopped chives, to garnish

MARINADE
150 ml/⅔ cup dry white wine
150 ml/⅔ cup apple cider vinegar
1 teaspoon finely chopped rosemary leaves

SAUCE
3 tablespoons Spanish extra virgin olive oil
1 onion, peeled and finely chopped
3 garlic cloves, peeled and finely chopped
1 carrot, peeled and finely chopped
½ green (bell) pepper, deseeded and finely chopped
½ red (bell) pepper, deseeded and finely chopped
50 g/scant ¼ cup tomato sauce (see page 93)
salt and freshly ground black pepper

SERVES 2

Talos de maíz con queso y txistorra

CORN FLATBREADS WITH CHEESE & SAUSAGE

It was in a caserío (traditional farmhouse) serving local food, not far from Vera de Vidasoa in Northern Navarra, where I was first offered a talo. A talo is a type of thin flatbread made with maize flour, not dissimilar to a Mexican tortilla. It has never been easy to grow wheat in 'green' Spain, so in the past maize flour talos were used in place of wheat flour bread, especially in Navarra.

From the caserío's kitchen came two hot talos. One was topped with slices of a melted local cheese, the other with a glorious piece of txistorra sausage. Today, talos have become a regular and welcome offering in many local markets and restaurants, served with a multitude of different toppings.

I have to say that I enjoy a talo most when piping hot, topped with nothing but some melting Idiazábal or Roncal cheese, served on a piece of parchment paper and eaten standing up while drinking a zurito (glass of red wine). Although I must confess that a talo filled with a good txistorra sausage, cooked in a pan set over a barbecue, is equally good. Txistorra is a very long and thin, fresh sausage made with quality pork meat, garlic and sweet smoked paprika.

350 g/12½ oz. maize flour,
  plus extra for dusting
250 ml/1 cup warm water
200 g/7 oz. txistorra (red sausages),
  each one cut into 4 or 5 pieces
150 g/5½ oz. Idiazábal or
  Roncal cheese, thinly sliced
Spanish olive oil, for greasing
salt

MAKES 8

Combine the maize flour and a pinch of salt in a mixing bowl. Slowly add the warm water, little by little, stirring first with a silicone spatula and then using one hand to work it into a rough dough. Transfer the dough to a clean work surface. Working first with one hand and then with both hands, knead it to a light and compact dough. Cover the dough in cling film/plastic wrap and rest in the fridge for about 30 minutes.

Remove from the dough from the fridge and cut it into 8 equal pieces. Lightly dust the work surface with maize flour. The less flour you use, the lighter the talos will be. Shape each piece of dough into a ball. Patting with your fingers and turning it over several times, form the dough into a flatbread that is as thin as possible but without tearing it.

Before cooking the flatbreads, prepare the sausage. Brush a small frying pan/skillet with olive oil and sauté the pieces of sausage for a few minutes. Transfer to a plate and keep warm.

Using a wide, flat frying pan (such as a crêpe pan), cook each flatbread for 2–3 minutes, turning only once. Keep warm while you cook the rest.

Wipe clean the pan with paper towels. Add the cheese and melt it over a low heat.

When ready to serve, place each flatbread on a piece of parchment paper, top with some of the melted cheese and several pieces of sausage.

Alubias negras de Tolosa
BLACK BEANS FROM EL FRONTON

In Guipúzcoa, 16 miles/27 km east of San Sebastián, is the town of Tolosa which is renowned, amongst other things, for a dish of alubias negras (black beans) grown in the local area. Not so long ago, these beans were included in the daily diet of farmers. Now, they are a delicacy that needs to be tasted in order to understand the reasons behind their popularity.

Definitely not light and summery, these beans make a rich dish. It is a serious Basque dish cooked with plenty of care and attention. Roberto Ruiz, chef at the El Fronton restaurant in Tolosa, is famed for making unbelievably good alubias. He uses the typical ingredients and yet somehow his alubias are lighter and even more delicious than the traditional recipe, if that were possible. 'Cooking the beans well is what it really matters,' he says. The beans, which are intensely black, can be cooked without soaking as long as they are from the last season's crop, otherwise they need to be soaked for a number of hours. In the UK, they can be purchased from Spanish food specialists or online. I always bring some home every year when returning to England by ferry from Bilbao.

Replicating Roberto's recipe without the correct ingredients is a challenge, especially the morcilla (black pudding/blood sausage). I love morcilla from Olano in the province of Alava, made with pig's blood, pork fat, onions, leeks, oregano and salt. It is difficult to buy outside the Basque Country, but I have found an excellent black pudding made in Scotland, which I buy from my local butcher in Wimbledon, London.

Although it is less traditional, I often serve this dish with young greens instead of cabbage.

500 g/1 lb. 2 oz. Tolosana black beans
5 tablespoons Spanish extra virgin olive oil, plus extra for drizzling
250 g/9 oz. morcilla (black pudding/blood sausage) with natural casing
½ large Savoy cabbage, washed, sliced and cut into thin strips
2 garlic cloves, peeled and finely chopped
piparras chillies/chiles, to serve
coarse sea salt, taste

SERVES 4

Put the beans into a deep saucepan or pot with two handles. Pour in enough water to cover the beans, then bring to the boil. Once boiling, reduce the heat, add 2 tablespoons of the olive oil and cook for 2 hours, or until the beans are tender. During the cooking time, add half a glass of cold water 3 or 4 times to the pan or pot to slow down the cooking process. Season with salt only when the beans are cooked, never before. Do not stir the beans during cooking, instead shake the pan from time to time to ensure the beans remain unbroken. (If you serve broken beans, Basques will know that you don't know how to cook them!)

To prepare the black pudding/blood sausage, bring a saucepan of water to the boil. Reduce the heat and add the black pudding to warm through. Using a sharp knife, make small incisions along the black pudding and, without breaking it apart, carefully cut it into slices.

Blanch the cabbage for a couple of minutes in pan of boiling water, then drain. Heat 3 tablespoons of the olive oil in a frying pan/skillet, add the garlic and sauté until it takes on a little colour. Add the cabbage to the pan and sauté for a minute or two.

When ready to serve, ladle the beans into deep soup plates, then divide the cabbage and black pudding between the bowls. Serve the piparras chillies/chiles alongside, drizzled with olive oil and seasoned with a pinch of coarse sea salt.

A TRADITIONAL ATTACHMENT

Recipes for fish & seafood

Fish & the fishermen

Imagine entering a restaurant and, on the hot plate of a cast-iron range in the open kitchen, you see two hake steaks, at least 5 cm/2 inches thick, cut from the centre of a 3 kg/6 lb. fish and on the bone. They are served slightly caramelised on the exterior, perfectly moist inside and dressed with a warm sauce made with olive oil, butter, lemon juice, garlic and parsley. *Merluza a la Hondarreña* (Hondarroa-style hake) was created at the Penalti restaurant and is typical of the town of Ondarroa in Vizcaya. This dish makes it easy to understand why Basques love fish.

Since medieval times, from the western border with the region of Cantabria to beyond Bayonne in France, Basques have built a line of colourful coastal towns and villages that look out onto the Cantabrian Sea. Sailors and expert navigators at heart, Basques were searching for fish, possible riches and a life of adventure beyond their Atlantic shores and towards the New World. On the Basque coast, surrounded by mountains and traditional houses painted white, green and red, I watch the arrival of the fishing vessels as they land their fresh cargo at the quays and then visit the auctions at the *lonja* (wholesale market) close by. I love the sea and I love fish.

I started travelling the Basque Country during my teens. My older brother was training as an officer in the merchant navy aboard the S.S. *Covadonga*. The ship regularly docked at Santurce, close to Bilbao. Every two months, my family would travel north from Madrid to visit him. We always stayed in a small hotel where my father, who was pescatarian, would order the *sopa de pescado y marisco* (seafood soup) and any dish with *merluza* (hake), which is something I still do myself when visiting that coast.

For those seeking a plate of the freshest fish cooked by people who truly understand it, the Basque Country guarantees treat after treat. Roasted in the oven, fried in a pan or cooked *a la brasa* (on the grill),

there are plenty of delicious choices. Basques love fish served with a good sauce and there are four main classics: the vibrant green *salsa verde* (parsley sauce), the complex red *vizcaína* (red onion and pepper sauce); the amazing light yellow *pil-pil* (olive oil and garlic sauce); and the intense black sauce made with squid or cuttlefish ink and served with contemporary fish and rice dishes.

Whether eating in smart restaurants, modest bars, *sidreras* (cider houses), *txokos* (gastronomic societies) or private homes, Basque cooking standards are equally high. Eating at a restaurant run by a *Hermandad de Pescadores* (fishermen's guild) located inside a port is another experience never to be missed. Not so long ago, I feasted at the picturesque port of Ondarribia in Guipúzcoa, very close to San Sebastián and the border with France. One of the daily specials was a starter of clams. To follow you could choose between squid in its own ink or a fresh bonito stew with potatoes and tomatoes known as *marmitako*. Always a tricky choice, for dessert was a tempting *torrija de la casa* (bread pudding) or a slice of *pastel Vasco* (Basque gâteau), baked just across the French border that morning. People were drinking cider, beer or *txakoli* (white wine). Before lunch I had a *zurito* (small glass of cool beer).

For me, the word *txipirón* (baby squid) brings back sweet memories of a week spent in Ondarroa researching the life and food of a retired fisherman.

Clockwise from top left: Ondarroa, a fishing village in the province of Biscay; fresh fish at market; the colourful Santiago Plaza in Pasai Donibane. Overleaf: Fishing boats in the port of Donostia-San Sebastián.

Almost every morning he would take his rowing boat out into the bay not far from his home to catch dozens of *txipirones* to cook or to share with friends or his family. Seeing him so efficiently cleaning these little squid, which is an art, preparing the vegetables needed, adding the wine and the ink at the right time. Being invited to taste such a marvellous dish is something that does not happen very often.

Regarding the Basques love and expertise with fish and shellfish, one could write a whole book full of stories. We could tell about cod, salted cod, anchovies fresh and preserved, *merluza de pintxo* (hake caught with line and hook), turbot, as it is prepared in Getaria, large tuna fish or smaller bonito, spider crab *a la donostiarra*, red mullet cooked in parchment paper. There are also clams cooked with plenty of wine, garlic and parsley, anchovies *al estilo de Bermeo* cooked in a large pot of hot olive oil with chillies and garlic which I saw prepared by fisherman on the beach. *Besugo* (large sea bream) is also very popular and in my family it occupies still now, a very special place at the Christmas table. It is totally delicious quite simply roasted with a couple of thin slices of lemon inserted under the skin, sprinkled with plenty of white wine and roasted potatoes.

There are two further dishes I must mention to do justice to this chapter: a plate of *angulas* and another of *kokotxas*. *Angulas* are elvers (minute transparent eels known as glass elvers). Long ago they disappeared from the Iberian Peninsula and are now imported mostly from the UK. In the Basque Country, they are considered one of the greatest delicacies to be eaten, especially during the Tamborrada, the drumming festival that takes place in January in San Sebastián. During the Tamborrada, elvers are traditionally served in all gastronomic societies and bars in small earthenware *cazuelitas*. They are cooked in olive oil, garlic and chilli pepper.

Kokotxas are very different, but equally valued by Basques. They are fresh or salted cheeks of hake or cod (hake are superior). For people who like gelatinous textures, *kokotxas* are really quite unique. In the *cazuelita*, the gelatine in the fish skin emulsifies with the oil and garlic to form a very special, delicate, creamy sauce with a great flavour following a method known as *pil-pil*. Simply put, whenever possible, I must have them.

Antxoas en papel
ANCHOVIES COOKED IN PAPER

Before I get on to the recipe, allow me to share a food memory that I will never forget. One day, sitting by a small beach in Getaria, I saw some fisherman cooking fresh anchovies in a large pot full of hot oil to which they had added some garlic and guindilla (fresh green chillies/chiles). Taking turns, each with a large slice of bread in hand, they added to the pot a handful of fresh anchovies. After a minute or so, they speared some anchovies from the pot with a fork and put them on the bread. I couldn't help looking on full of envy. That was noticed, so they offered me a taste, as well as a small glass of the local txakoli wine produced just a few kilometres away from where we sat. It was such an unbelievable experience.

Fresh anchovies are not only delicious and inexpensive, they are full of goodness. In Spain, you can find them everywhere, but they may be difficult to source elsewhere because of their short shelf life – they do need to be eaten when very fresh. Although it is not quite the same, if you cannot find fresh anchovies, use very fresh small sardines, which are equally lovely.

4 tablespoons Spanish extra virgin olive oil, plus extra for greasing
1 large onion, peeled and finely chopped
4 garlic cloves, peeled and chopped
100 g/3½ oz. mushrooms, cleaned and sliced
juice of ½ lemon
50 ml/scant ¼ cup white wine
1 tablespoon chopped flat-leaf parsley, plus extra to garnish
1 kg/2¼ lb. fresh anchovies (or fresh small sardines), cleaned and gutted
100 g/½ cup/1 stick butter
salt and freshly ground black pepper

SERVES 6

Preheat the oven to 180°C/160°C fan/350°F/Gas 4.

Heat the olive oil in a frying pan/skillet over a medium heat. Add the onion and garlic, then cook for 5 minutes or until soft. Add the sliced mushrooms and cook for a further 5 minutes. Remove the pan from the heat and add the lemon juice, white wine and chopped parsley. Season to taste with salt and black pepper.

Tear off 6 squares of parchment paper, large enough to enclose the anchovies in a parcel. Brush one side of each sheet with a little oil. Divide the anchovies equally between the sheets, placing them in the centre of the paper. Add the mushroom mixture to each bundle of anchovies, then top with a little butter. Bring the sides of the sheet up over the anchovies and scrunch the parchment paper tightly together to seal the fish in a parcel. Place the parcels on a baking sheet.

Bake the fish parcels in the preheated oven for about 10 minutes. When ready, place the paper parcels on individual plates to serve. The parcels may release some hot steam, so take care when opening the parcels.

Bacalao Club Ranero
SALT COD CLUB RANERO

Fish is a passion in Euskadi, especially in the provinces bordering the Cantabrian sea. Dishes prepared with cod and hake, in particular, never go out of fashion. Some unique recipes need a little attention and an understanding of how to make a perfect emulsion, similar to a homemade mahonesa sauce but served hot.

Two of these recipes – bacalao al pil-pil and bacalao Club Ranero – are perfect examples of a cooking technique in which olive oil, garlic and the natural gelatin in fish skin combine to make a perfect emulsion, helped by agitating the pan while cooking. If you just make the sauce, this dish is called bacalao al pil-pil. However, if you continue and add the sautéed vegetables, it becomes bacalao Club Ranero. The addition of the vegetables to the sauce lightens the whole dish in a beautiful way.

Traditionally this dish is prepared in a cazuela (earthenware pot), but I make it in a wide, deep metal pan with two handles. This dish is not the same made with fresh cod as the sauce does not become so silky and, well, so wonderful!

4 salt cod fillets (each weighing 200 g/
    7 oz.), with skin left on
300 ml/1¼ cups Spanish olive oil, plus
    an extra 2 tablespoons for the onions
3 garlic cloves, peeled and sliced
1 white onion, peeled and finely chopped
1 courgette/zucchini, peeled and chopped
500 g/1 lb. 2 oz. fresh tomatoes, peeled
    and chopped
250 g/9 oz. green (bell) peppers,
    deseeded and chopped
3 teaspoons choricero pepper paste
hunks of good bread, to serve

SERVES 4

Rinse the salt cod fillets under cold running water and pat dry with paper towels. Place in a large saucepan and cover with plenty of fresh water. Leave to soak for 24 hours, changing the water every 8 hours. Rinse again under running water, then remove any fish bones.

Heat the olive oil in a wide pan with handles – it needs to be large enough to cook all the fillets without them touching. Add the garlic to the pan and gently sauté until it takes on a light colour. Remove the garlic from the pan and set aside to use again later.

Place the fish in the pan in a single layer, skin side up, and cook over a low heat for 8–10 minutes. Once cooked, drain off half the warm oil from the pan into a heatproof jug/pitcher and set aside to use again later.

Holding the pan by both handles, move it in a continuous circular motion over the heat so that the fish shifts around in the pan. Slowly pour the warm oil back into the pan, little by little, while continuing to move it around. Return the reserved garlic to the pan, too. White droplets of gelatin from the fish skin will appear on the surface of the oil. Continue agitating the pan to help the warm oil to emulsify into a thick sauce.

Heat 2 tablespoons of olive oil in a frying pan/skillet. Add the onion and cook until soft and translucent. Add the rest of the vegetables to the pan along with the choricero pepper paste and cook for about 10 minutes.

Using a slotted spoon, remove the vegetables from the pan and spoon them over the fish with the sauce. Serve with some good bread alongside.

Filetitos finos de bacalao salado en casa con salsa de tomate y hierbas aromáticas

HOME-SALTED COD WITH A TOMATO SALSA

Influenced by the informative book El Bacalao Biología y Gastronomía by Emilio Gonzalez Soto, I have added this very tasty modern recipe for home-salted cod. This is not a difficult dish to prepare, but it does take time. If you prefer not to salt the cod yourself, ask one of the Spanish specialist food shops to sell you some vacuum-packed bacalao that is ready to use. The only thing you then need to do is to make the tomato salsa and prepare the fresh herbs.

Lay the cod loin on top of a thin layer of sea salt spread over the base of a rectangular glass or ceramic dish. Completely cover the fish with another thin layer of sea salt. Cover the dish with foil and place a weight on top. (I use another slightly smaller glass or ceramic dish full of ceramic baking beans.) Transfer the dish to the fridge and chill for about 1½ hours.

Remove the cod loin from the dish and brush off the salt. Rinse the fish under cold running water, remove the skin and pat dry with paper towels. Wrap the fish in parchment paper and place in the fridge for a further few hours to dry out and slightly harden. Once dried, using a sharp knife, cut the salted cod loin into very thin slices.

The salted cod can be used at this point, however I like to cover the slices with milk and leave them to soak for a further few hours. Drain the cod slices, discarding the milk, and set aside.

Fill a saucepan with boiling water and a bowl with iced water. Prick the tomato skins several times with a wooden skewer. Blanch the tomatoes in the boiling water for just a minute, then transfer them to the iced water. Remove the skins and seeds from the tomatoes, then chop the flesh into very small cubes.

Dress the diced tomatoes with some olive oil, sherry vinegar and a touch of sea salt, cover and leave to rest in the fridge for an hour or so. Pour some of the juices from the tomato salsa over the cod slices and let them rest again.

Arrange the cod slices over a serving platter. Spoon the tomato salsa on top, then scatter over the chopped olives and mixed herbs. Drizzle with a little more olive oil and season with black pepper.

500 g/1 lb. 2 oz. cod loin, skin left on
sea salt, for salting the cod
milk, for soaking the cod

TOMATO SALSA
300 g/10½ oz. ripe tomatoes on the vine
Spanish extra virgin olive oil, to taste
sherry vinegar, to taste
sea salt, to taste

TO SERVE
handful of Spanish cured black olives
    (available from specialist shops)
handful of mixed herbs (I use mint,
    dill and flat-leaf parsley), to garnish
Spanish extra virgin olive oil, for drizzling
freshly ground black pepper

SERVES 4–6

Bacalao fresco con crema de coliflor y piperrada

FRESH COD, CAULIFLOWER PURÉE & BASQUE PEPPERS

Cod, mostly salted, is used in many Basque recipes, both traditional and modern. The Basques have a long history of scouring the North Atlantic Ocean for their beloved fish. Before refrigeration, they then needed to preserve the cod during their journey back to Iberia. Salt, which is plentiful in Spain, was the obvious solution.

Until fairly recently, fresh cod was seldom seen in Spanish markets... or truly appreciated, for that matter. Even today, Basques often buy cod which has been salted. They hold the secret to making it taste delicious: a number of original sauces that I have included in other recipes. Even so, encouraged by today's chefs, people are looking for an alternative to salt cod. As a response, I am including this recipe for fresh cod which uses a method of preparation that brings back, in a contemporary way, some of the attraction of lightly salted cod. In Spain, you can find bacalao already desalted or partially desalted which is used more and more, especially by professional cooks in some exceptionally good recipes.

30 g/1 oz. salt
4 cod fillets (each weighing 100 g/
    3½ oz.), deboned and with skin left on
Spanish olive oil, for frying
1 quantity of piperrada
    (Basque peppers, see page 30)
freshly ground black pepper

CAULIFLOWER PURÉE
250 g/9 oz. cauliflower, cut into florets
100 ml/scant ½ cup whole/full-fat milk
100 ml/scant ½ cup double/heavy cream
splash of white wine vinegar
fine sea salt

SERVES 4

Dissolve the salt in a large bowl with 1 litre/4 cups to make a saline solution. Add the cod fillets to the bowl and leave to soak for 1 hour. Remove the fish from the saline solution and gently pat dry with paper towels. Set aside.

Place the cauliflower florets in a large saucepan. Pour in the milk, then top up with water until the cauliflower is just covered. Season with salt. Cook over a medium heat until tender. Drain the cauliflower, removing as much of the cooking liquid as possible, and leave to cool. Once cool, put the cooked cauliflower in a blender and blitz before adding the cream and blitzing again to make a smooth purée. Season with salt to taste, adding a little white wine vinegar, if needed.

When ready to serve, brush the cod with oil. Cook the fish in a frying pan/skillet over a medium heat for 3–4 minutes on each side or until it takes on a little colour.

Spoon some of the cauliflower purée onto each plate, then place the cod on top. Divide the piperrada between the plates, then finish by drizzling over a few drops of oil from the piperrada sauce and seasoning with some black pepper.

Txipirones en su tinta
BABY SQUID IN ITS OWN INK

Squid served in its own ink is a dish that was recorded by Francisco Martinez Montiño, chef to Philip II and Philip III in seventeenth-century Spain. It was, and still is, loved by Basques, especially during the summer months when the favoured small txipirones (baby squid) are in season. The late Basque chef José Juan Castillo, wrote in 2000, 'Caught by a hook and cooked the same day for greatest freshness, Cantabrian squid shines ever brighter when exalted in a dressing of its own ink, along with onion, peeled and diced tomato, green pepper, fish stock and txakoli (white wine), all to the taste of whoever cooks and enjoys it.'

You can buy txipirones and clean them yourself or, if you prefer, ask your fishmonger to do it for you. Keep the tentacles and wings as they are needed to stuff the squid. As the ink sacs of baby squid are so small, you will probably need to buy extra sachets of fresh or frozen ink from a good fishmonger.

30 baby squid
1 sachet of squid ink
500 ml/2 cups Spanish extra virgin
 olive oil, as needed
5 large onions, peeled and chopped
6 garlic cloves, peeled and chopped
3 green (bell) peppers, deseeded and
 chopped
3 tomatoes, peeled and finely chopped
100 ml/scant ½ cup red wine
100 ml/scant ½ cup txakoli white wine
salt and freshly ground black pepper
boiled white rice, to serve

SERVES 6

To clean the squid, pull out the innards from each one, including the hard, transparent back bone. Keep the tentacles and wings. Before discarding the innards, very carefully remove the ink sacs and set aside them aside in a small bowl filled with a little water. Using your fingers, release all the ink from the sacs. Once it has dissolved in the water, discard the empty ink sacs.

Clean the squid bodies, tentacles and wings under cold running water. Remove any membranes and, using your finger, turn the body of each squid inside out. (Turning the body inside out prevents the stuffing coming out during cooking.) Peel and chop the tentacles and wings as best you can, then use them to stuff the bodies.

Heat a couple of tablespoons of olive oil in a frying pan/skillet and sauté the stuffed squid for 1–2 minutes or until they take on a little colour. Transfer the squid to a large, but not too deep saucepan.

Wipe clean the frying pan with paper towels. Heat 3 tablespoons of the olive oil in the cleaned pan, add the onions and gently cook until translucent. Add a couple of tablespoons of boiling water and continue cooking until the onions are very soft.

In a separate pan, gently cook the garlic and green (bell) peppers in another 2 tablespoons of olive oil. Add the tomatoes to the pan along with the cooked onions. Transfer this mixture (sofrito) to a bowl. Deglaze the frying pan with the red wine and the same quantity of water and pour the liquid into the same bowl.

Add the white wine to the squid ink already dissolved in water. Pour this squid ink mixture over the sofrito, then transfer to a blender. Blitz, then pass it through a fine-mesh sieve/strainer to make a smooth sauce.

Pour the sauce over the squid and gently simmer for about 1 hour or until the squid is tender and the flavours of the sauce have mingled. Season to taste and serve with rice.

Marmita de salmón fresco
ONE-PAN SALMON IN A VEGETABLE SAUCE

Years ago my mother took me to Zalacain in Madrid. Specialising in Basque cuisine, in 1987, Zalacain was the first Spanish restaurant to obtain three Michelin stars. We enjoyed two or three different dishes, including a fresh salmon marmita that my mother later reproduced at home to perfection. She loved the simplicity of the fish dish and how it was made with such care, bringing out the best in each ingredient. Served in small, dark ceramic dishes, it not only looked fantastic but it tasted even better.

First, prepare the fish stock. Place the fish head and bones, along with all the vegetables and herbs, in a large stock pot. Pour over 4 litres/quarts water, place over a medium to high heat and bring to a boil. Skim off any foam that appears on the surface; keep doing this until the stock stays clear. Once the stock starts boiling, add a little cold water, then keep the heat low, gently simmer the stock for at least 30 minutes or until reduced by one-third. Leave the stock to cool, then clarify it by straining through a sieve/strainer that is lined with a coffee filter paper. Adjust the seasoning with salt to taste. Set aside the 300 ml/1¼ cups of stock needed for the sauce, then store any leftover stock in the fridge or freezer to use later in another recipe.

For the sauce, melt half the butter in a deep saucepan and sauté the shallot until soft. Add the rest of the vegetables and cook for a further few minutes. Pour in the wine and reserved stock and cook until the vegetables are almost tender. Transfer to a food processor or blender and blitz until smooth. For a smoother sauce, pass it through a fine-mesh sieve/strainer. Place the sauce back in the pan and keep warm.

In a deep frying pan/skillet, sauté the salmon in a little olive oil until it takes on some colour but remains slightly pink inside. Pour over the warm sauce and gently cook for a few minutes, then add the rest of the butter and let it melt into the sauce. Serve with fried potatoes and some steamed greens.

500 g/1 lb. 2 oz. thick salmon fillets, skin removed, cut into large cubes
Spanish mild olive oil, for frying
fried potatoes, to serve
steamed greens, to serve

FISH STOCK
750 g/1 lb. 10 oz. white fish head and bones, including the salmon head from the fillets
1 small carrots, peeled and cut into thick rounds
2 celery stalks/ribs, cleaned and cut into thick rounds
1 leek, cleaned and cut into thick rounds
1 small onion, peeled and roughly chopped
1 bay leaf
few sprigs of flat-leaf parsley
salt, to taste

SAUCE
60 g/¼ cup/½ stick butter
1 shallot, peeled and finely chopped
1 medium courgette/zucchini, peeled and chopped into small cubes
1 medium leek, cleaned and cut into thin matchsticks
1 medium carrot, peeled and cut into thin matchsticks
100 ml/scant ½ cup dry white wine
300 ml/1¼ cups fish stock (see above)
salt and freshly ground black pepper

SERVES 4

Merluza en salsa verde

HAKE IN PARSLEY SAUCE

Whenever you mention the name of this dish, the Basques will smile with pleasure. They love merluza (hake) and they adore it in one of the most characteristic Basque recipes, especially when it is cooked in a sociedad gastronómica (gastronomic society). Traditionally, this dish is prepared in a cazuela (earthenware pot), but I tend to use a wide, deep metal pan with two handles that is large enough to cook the fish in a single layer. As with the Bacalao Club Ranero (see page 111), the natural gelatine in the fish skin emulsifies with the olive oil and garlic and, when agitated by swirling the pan, it transforms into a silky sauce. The fresh clams are added just a couple of minutes before the hake is ready to serve, but you can always leave them out if you prefer.

1 kg/2¼ lb. hake, cut into 4 large slices and with skin left on
200 ml/scant 1 cup Spanish extra virgin olive oil
4 garlic cloves, peeled and sliced
100 ml/scant ½ cup dry white wine
50 ml/scant ¼ cup fish stock (see page 10)
1 tablespoon finely chopped flat-leaf parsley
16 live clams (cleaned and prepared in the same ways as mussels, see page 26, optional)
salt

SERVES 4

Sprinkle the skin of the fish with a little salt and let it rest in the fridge for a couple of hours to extract any moisture.

Heat the olive oil in a wide pan with handles – it needs to be large enough to cook all the fillets without them touching. Add the garlic to the pan and gently sauté until it takes on a light colour. Remove the garlic from the pan and drain off about half of the oil into a heatproof jug/pitcher. Set aside both to use again later.

Using the same pan and the remaining warm oil, place the fish in the pan in a single layer, skin side up, and increase the heat slightly. In a few minutes, white droplets of gelatine from the fish skin will appear on the surface of the oil. This is the moment to start moving the pan. Holding the pan by both handles, move it in a continuous circular motion over the heat so that the fish shifts around in the pan –do this for a minute or two. Return the reserved garlic to the pan and continue agitating the pan to help the warm oil emulsify into a thick sauce.

To thin the sauce, add some of the reserved olive oil, white wine and stock. Add the chopped parsley and cook for a few minutes until the sauce has fully emulsified and has a lovely creamy texture and a pale green colour. If you are using the clams, add them now, cover the pan, and cook for a further two minutes or until the clams have opened. Discard any clams that do not open.

Marmitako de bonito de Jesús

JESUS'S BONITO MARMITAKO

Marmitako is derived from the word marmita, the term for a type of cooking pot, and so marmitako means 'from the pot'. There are many different recipes in the Basque Country for this dish, which is prepared in the summer months when Atlantic bonito (Sarda sarda) is at its best. To celebrate the Basque's unwavering passion for fish, marmitako competitions take place in numerous coastal locations. Back in the 1990s, when filming the BBC Television series, Spain on a Plate, Jesús was the cook on a fishing boat called La Nécora. While we were out at sea, he prepared the most wonderful marmitako in the boat's galley. We were invited to eat with the crew on deck; spoons in hands, we ate Jesús's tasty dish with slices of very good bread – a meal never to be forgotten. Jesús did not roast the peppers beforehand, but I find doing so adds something even more special to the finished dish.

1 kg/2¼ lb. Atlantic bonito (or skipjack tuna), skinned and cut into cubes
2 red (bell) peppers
2 green (bell) peppers
Spanish extra virgin olive oil, for frying
6 garlic cloves, peeled and chopped
1 onion, peeled and finely chopped
2 teaspoons sweet smoked paprika
500 g/1 lb. 2 oz. tomatoes, peeled, deseeded and finely chopped
1 green chilli/chile pepper, deseeded and chopped
1 kg/2¼ lb. potatoes, peeled and cut into cubes the same size as the bonito
salt, to taste
slices of toasted bread, to serve

SERVES 6

Season the bonito with a little salt and set aside.

Preheat the oven to 180°C/160°C fan/350°F/Gas 4.

Put the red and green peppers in a roasting tin/sheet pan and roast in the preheated oven until their skins can be easily removed. Peel and slice the peppers, discarding the stalks and seeds. Heat 2 tablespoons olive oil in a frying pan/skillet. Add the roasted peppers to the pan and one of the garlic cloves, then sauté for a few minutes or until tender. Set aside.

In a separate, larger frying pan, gently sauté the onions and the remaining garlic until soft. Increase the heat and cook for a further couple of minutes, stirring continuously, until they take on a light colour. Move the onion and garlic to one side of the pan, then add the paprika and cook stirring, to avoid burning, which can easily happen. Add the tomatoes and chilli/chile to the pan with the onions, then cook for 10 minutes, mixing everything together. Add the roasted peppers and cook for a further 5–6 minutes. Set aside.

Place the potatoes in a large saucepan and cover with cold lightly salted water. (Remember that the bonito is already salted.) Bring the water to the boil. When the potatoes are almost cooked (no need to drain them) add the bonito to the pan, followed by the pepper and tomato sauce. Stir only once to avoid breaking the potatoes and cook for a final 5 minutes. Serve with good bread.

Lubina a la pimienta verde
SEA BASS WITH GREEN PEPPERCORNS

Created by Pedro Subijana, one of the founders of La Nueva Cocina Vasca (New Basque Cuisine), sea bass with green peppercorns has become a classic Basque dish. Pedro is the chef patron of Akelarre, the acclaimed restaurant in San Sebastián with three Michelin stars. At Akelarre, this dish is served with a pastry in the shape of a fish. I have made some simple pastry sticks using ready-rolled puff pastry for convenience.

knob of unsalted butter
3 tablespoons Spanish extra virgin
   olive oil
1 shallot, peeled and finely chopped
4 sea bass fillets (about 800 g/1¾ lb.
   total weight), with skin left on
50 g/4½ tablespoons green
   peppercorns
3 tablespoons brandy
200 ml/scant 1 cup single/light cream
1 sheet of ready-rolled puff pastry,
   cut into thin strips and baked
   according to the packet
   instructions (optional)
fresh or frozen peas, to serve

SERVES 4

Preheat the oven to 200°C/180°C fan/400°F/Gas 6.

Heat the butter and olive oil in an ovenproof frying pan/skillet. Add the shallot and sauté until softened. Place the sea bass fillets on top of the shallots and add the peppercorns. Flame the dish with the brandy, then stir in the cream. Place the pan in the preheated oven and cook for 6–7 minutes.

Transfer the sea bass to a warmed dish, leaving the sauce behind in the pan. Place the pan over a high heat and quickly reduce the sauce. When ready, spoon a puddle of sauce onto each serving plate and place a sea bass fillet on top. Serve with more sauce, the peas and puff pastry sticks, if using.

Chipirones a la luzienne
LUZIENNE-STYLE BABY SQUID

This is another very popular dish prepared in the French Basque provinces. Although the original recipe calls for txipirones (baby squid), the dish is equally good made with large squid.

4–5 tablespoons Spanish extra
   virgin olive oil
2 onions, peeled and chopped
5 garlic cloves, peeled and chopped
2 green (bell) peppers, peeled,
   deseeded and sliced
1 tablespoon tomato purée/paste
1 kg/2¼ lb. baby squid, cleaned and
   prepared (see page 117)
1 fresh espelette pepper, sliced
3 large tomatoes, peeled and diced
salt

SERVES 4

Heat 2–3 tablespoons of the olive oil in a large, deep frying pan/skillet. Add the onions, garlic and green (bell) peppers and sauté until almost soft. Add the tomato purée/paste and cook, stirring, for about 10–12 minutes.

Meanwhile, in a separate large frying pan, heat the remaining olive oil. Working in batches, sauté the squid for just a couple of minutes.

Stir the cooked onions and peppers into pan with the squid and gently cook for 30 minutes. Add the espelette pepper and diced tomatoes and cook for a further few minutes. Taste and adjust the seasoning with salt, if needed.

When ready, spoon some of the onion, pepper and tomato sauce into individual serving bowls, then divide the squid between the bowls before serving.

Ttoro, una cazuela de pescado y marisco de St. Jean de Luz

BASQUE SEAFOOD STEW FROM ST. JEAN DE LUZ

Whenever I travel to San Sebastián and have plenty of time to spare, I fly to Bilbao, hire a car and take the uniquely Cantabrian coastal road that is, more often than not, battered by a magnificent sea often aggravated by the capricious weather. There are so many ports to stop at, enjoy the view and eat something local: Ondarroa, Lequeitio, Motrico, Getaria...

Other times I fly to Biarritz, which gives me the perfect excuse to stay a few days, travel around the French Basque provinces and enjoy a traditional dish or two. One of my favourites is ttoro, a substantial seafood stew seasoned with espelette pepper from the fishing port of St. Jean de Luz. Espelette is a variety of Capsicum anuum cultivated in the French commune of Espelette, in the Pyrénées-Atlantiques and is appellation-controlled. The powdered form provides a subtle heat and can be purchased in some supermarkets and online.

When making ttoro yourself, ask your fishmonger for Scorpion fish, if possible, though I often use gurnard as an alternative. Gurnard is not only perfect for making stock, it has an excellent texture for using in stews, such as this one.

First, make the stock. Heat a little olive oil in a large saucepan, add the scorpion fish heads and sauté for about 5 minutes. Add the onion, garlic, red (bell) pepper and chilli/chile and cook for about 5 minutes. Add the tomatoes and bouquet garni, stir again, before pouring in the wine and 350 ml/1½ cups water. Bring to the boil, reduce the heat and simmer for 30 minutes, skimming off any foam that appears on the surface. Strain the stock through a fine-mesh sieve/strainer into a shallow, large ovenproof dish, season with the espelette pepper, salt and black pepper. Set aside until needed.

Preheat the oven to 180°C/160°C fan/350°F/Gas 4.

Season all the fish with plenty of salt and black pepper, then lightly coat with the flour. Heat the remaining olive oil and fry the fish for 2–3 minutes on each side or until it has taken on a light colour. Arrange the fish in the ovenproof dish with the stock, then add the prawns/shrimp and mussels. Cook in the preheated oven for about 5 minutes or until the prawns are just cooked (but not overcooked) and mussels have opened. Serve with hot garlic bread.

100 ml/scant ½ cup Spanish olive oil

2 scorpion fish (or gurnard), cleaned, heads removed (and reserved), then flesh cut into chunks

1 large onion, peeled and chopped

2 garlic cloves, peeled and crushed

1 red (bell) pepper, deseeded and chopped

1 red fresh chilli/chile, deseeded and halved

400 g/14 oz. tomatoes, chopped

1 bouquet garni

300 ml/1¼ cups dry white wine

1 teaspoon piment d'Espelette (espelette pepper)

1 kg/2½ lb. hake fillets, with skin left on

2 large red mullets, cleaned, heads removed and cut into large chunks

1 monkfish tail, cut into chunks

2 tablespoons plain/all-purpose flour

14 large raw prawns/jumbo shrimp in their shells

14 large mussels, washed and beards removed (see page 26)

salt and freshly ground black pepper

slices of hot garlic bread, to serve

SERVES 6

El budin de merluza de mi familia

MY FAMILY'S HAKE BUDIN

This is one of the recipes my grandmother prepared as an appetiser for the most important family event of the year, Nochebuena (Christmas Eve). She called it a budin. While researching Basque food in the late 1980s, I found that budin was a much-celebrated recipe prepared in towns and villages all along the Bay of Biscay, in Asturias, Cantabria and the Basque Country. What I did not know is that chef Juan Mari Arzak based his celebrated pastel de kabrarroka (scorpion fish) on the original hake recipe, refining it in the 1970s and substituting the hake for scorpion fish. While Juan Mari's recipe went on to become an icon of La Nueva Cocina Vasca (New Basque Cuisine) and it is undoubtedly delicious, I have decided to share my family's original recipe, which I feel is equally great. As it has a fine texture, similar to pâté, it can also be served on small toasts, as a pintxo, with a little mahonesa sauce and a black olive on top.

First, prepare the mahonesa sauce following the directions on page 64. Set aside.

Cook the carrot and leek in a saucepan of boiling salted water until tender. Add the hake and cook for about 8 minutes, until the flesh easily flakes. Transfer the fish to a plate, then strain and store any leftover stock in the fridge or freezer to use later in another recipe.

When cool enough to handle, remove the skin and bones from the hake, then carefully flake the flesh. Place the flaked hake, eggs, tomato sauce and cream in a food processor and blitz until smooth (or leave a little chunkier if you prefer). Season with plenty of salt and black pepper.

Preheat the oven to 150°C/130°C fan/300°F/Gas 2.

Grease an ovenproof dish with the butter. Add the breadcrumbs in a thin layer to coat the base and sides of the dish. (This prevents the budin sticking to the dish.) Scrape the hake mixture into the dish and place in a deep roasting tray. Half-fill the tray with hot water and place in the preheated oven to cook for about 1 hour.

Remove the tray from the oven and let the budin cool. Once cool, remove from the dish and cover with mahonesa sauce. Serve on a bed of leaves dressed with extra virgin olive oil, salt and a few drops of sherry vinegar with some toasted bread and olives alongside.

1 carrot, peeled and chopped
1 leek, cleaned and chopped
500 g/1 lb. 2 oz. hake, on the bone, cut from the centre of the fish, with the skin left on
3 large/US extra-large eggs
2 tablespoons tomato sauce (see page 93)
200 ml/scant 1 cup double/heavy cream
1 tablespoon unsalted butter
1 tablespoon very fine breadcrumbs
salt and freshly ground black pepper
toasted bread and olives, to serve

MAHONESA SAUCE
500 ml/2 cups sunflower oil
2 medium/US large eggs
few drops lemon juice
few drops orange juice
sherry vinegar, to taste
salt, to taste

SERVES 8

Arroz con almejas
RICE WITH CLAMS

During one of my visits to San Sebastián, I was invited to have lunch in a classic sociedad gastronómica (gastronomic society) where my dear friend, the late José Juan Castillo, chef of chefs, prepared arroz con almejas (rice with clams), a classic Basque dish. Even though it was nothing fancy and inexpensive, I can still remember the flavour of the clam sauce. What made the dish was an understanding of what could be achieved with very few, simple but high-quality ingredients, which is something often only great cooks appear to master. The only thing needed to complete the dish is good bread to mop up the delicious sauce.

José Juan never gave quantities for his recipes, so here is my best effort to replicate his dish, of which I very much hope he would have approved. He insisted that using the most expensive clams was not necessary; very fresh, small clams, which are good value, are perfect for this dish. This dish uses arroz Calasparra, a variety of short-grain rice grown exclusively in the Calasparra region that is used for paella as the grains soak up a lot of moisture – remember, this rice does not need to be washed before using. If you cannot find Spanish Calasparra rice, then Arborio is a suitable alternative. This is a rice dish somewhere between what we Spanish call caldoso (soupy) and meloso (creamy). I like to serve it with plenty of crusty bread on the side.

RICE
4 tablespoons Spanish olive oil
4 garlic cloves, peeled and finely
  chopped
400 g/2 cups Calasparra rice
  (short-grain Spanish paella rice)
1 litre/4 cups boiling water
sea salt, to taste

CLAMS
splash of Spanish olive oil
4 garlic cloves, peeled and finely
  chopped
16 live clams (cleaned and prepared
  in the same ways as mussels,
  see page 26, optional)
2 small dried cayenne peppers
handful of flat-leaf parsley, roughly
  chopped

SERVES 4

To prepare the rice, heat the olive oil in a large saucepan. When the oil is hot (but not smoking), add the garlic and sauté until soft, but do not to let the garlic take on any colour. Add the rice to the pan, stir for a minute or so, then pour in the boiling water to cover the rice. Season with a little sea salt. Bring to the boil, then reduce the heat and let simmer, uncovered, over medium heat for about 18–20 minutes until tender. (You will not be required to drain the rice.)

Meanwhile, heat a splash of olive oil in a separate saucepan. Add the garlic and cook for 1 minute, then add the clams. Shake the pan before pouring in enough boiling water to just cover the clams. Shake the pan again and let the clams open – this only takes a moment. Discard any clams that do not open. Transfer the clams to a plate, leaving the juices behind.

Using a ladle, slowly add the soupy rice to the pan with the clam juices. Add the dried cayenne peppers, shaking the pan to combine all the flavours and let sit for 5 minutes. Remove the cayenne peppers and then scatter in the chopped parsley before serving.

FROM THE MOUNTAINS & VALLEYS

Cooking meat & sausage

Meat: Asadors, chuletas & more

I once flew to Bilbao with a friend who was writing an article about meat; they were interested in why Basque meat was in such demand by chefs in London and around Britain. We visited a number of markets in Bilbao, a farm in a magnificent valley not far from the city, and some restaurants famed for the quality of their meat. Eventually we found a restaurant we both adored. As enthusiastic meat eaters, we are unlikely to forget it. The restaurant was an *asador* (grill house) in Deusto, the district where the university of Bilbao is located. As we opened the glass front door to the establishment, we were inspired by huge, old-fashioned butcher's cooling cabinets where a number of impressive *chuletas* (T-bone steaks) hung, the best that money could buy. The various shades of red gave clear evidence of their different periods of ageing; old and not so young beef (ternera or vaca) and the very pricy *buey* (ox meat).

Inside the butcher's cabinets, we could also see some *chuletillas* (lamb chops) and two or three different types of *morcilla* (black pudding/blood sausage). As we were shown to our table, we could also see two large *parrillas* (metal grills) angled over hot charcoals where expert *parrilleros* were doing a fantastic job. The menu was short but tempting: there was meat, even more meat, salads and a few well-known desserts. The wine list was long and also tempting with plenty of Riojas, Riberas and Navarras, mostly red of course. We ordered two *pintxos* of *morcilla vasca* with sweet and sour red onions on top, a *tortilla de bacalao* (salt cod omelette) and a *chuleta*, which people wrongly call a *chuletón*. *Chuleta* in the Basque Country is a large T-bone steak. It is vital the *chuleta* is properly cooked, which means rare on the inside but slightly burnt on the outside.

There are a number of different types of *morcilla* found in the Basque Country. I am partial to the *morcilla dulce*, which is slightly sweet made with pig's blood, pork meat, vegetables, raisins, spices and pine nuts. The *mondejus* is a classic type of pudding from the area of Goierri in Guipúzcoa, but it is not black, rather it is a creamy colour as it is stuffed with onions, leeks, eggs and spices.

Basques love lamb, which is excellent in the whole of the greater region of the Basque Country. Here, since ancient times, mountains and valleys everywhere seem to be populated by hundreds of little white dots, which are sheep feeding on the rich pastures. It is not surprising that recipes cooked with lamb have enriched the cuisine of this region both in Spain and France. In this book I have included several recipes with lamb such as the popular *cordero al chilindrón* (slow-cooked lamb stew) and the original *cordero con anchoas y alcaparras* (roasted shoulder of lamb cooked with anchovies and capers).

Even though I am well aware that not everyone is keen on eating the meat of very young animals, I could not leave this chapter without mentioning a true speciality from Navarra: the *gorrin*, a young suckling pig that is roasted to perfection. Also from Navarra is *txistorra*, an uncured, thin, red sausage that is quite addictive, especially when eaten in a hot *talo*, a traditional flatbread made with maize flour.

Clockwise from top left: a view of the Aralar mountain range; a Basque shepherd and his flock; morcilla (blood sausages) hanging at the butchers; vineyards in La Rioja; chuletas on the grill; cuts of meat showcased at Asador Sugarra, Bilbao. Overleaf: sheep graze on Jaizkibel mountain.

Cerdo Ibérico marinado y asado con vino de Rioja tinto, laurel y clavos de olor

IBÉRICO PORK LOIN ROASTED IN RED WINE, BAY LEAVES & CLOVES

This recipe calls for any cut of fresh pork, but I like to prepare it with Ibérico pork loin. Wherever you are in Spain today, Ibérico meat has become a star in the firmament of Basque food. This is another celebratory recipe I love to prepare for festive days and family reunions. I learned the recipe from someone I knew in Madrid who was originally from Tolosa.

The day before, put the pork loin in a large non-reactive bowl. Pour over the wine and add the onion, carrots, leeks, garlic, bay leaves and cloves. Season with some salt and black pepper, then cover the bowl and leave the pork to marinate overnight.

The next day, remove the pork from the marinade and place the meat in a roasting tin/sheet pan. Strain the marinade, discarding the vegetables, bay leaves and cloves. Set aside the marinade.

Preheat the oven to 180°C/160°C fan/350°F/Gas 4.

Cover the pork with foil, then roast in the preheated oven for about 1½ hours. Remove the foil and return the meat uncovered to the oven and roast until the pork fat takes on a golden colour.

Meanwhile, prepare the fruit purée. Peel the apples and stone/pit the plums, then chop both into wedges. Pour the wine into a jug/pitcher and stir in the sugar until dissolved. Melt the butter in a saucepan. Add the chopped fruit, orange peel and wine mixture to the pan. Reduce the heat and cook very slowly until the fruit becomes tender, releases it juices and those juices have reduced by one-third. Set aside.

Once the pork has cooked, set it aside to rest while you make a red wine sauce from the reserved marinade and the meat juices in the bottom of the roasting tin. Combine the marinade and juices in a small sauce over a medium heat, bring the mixture to the boil for at least 5 minutes or until it has reduced by two-thirds. Beat in a knob/pat of cold butter at the end to give the sauce a glossy richness.

Thinly slice the pork, then serve with the red wine sauce, fruit purée and some watercress.

1.5 kg/3¼ lb. pork loin
750 ml/3 cups Rioja crianza red wine
1 large onion, chopped
2 carrots, peeled and chopped
2 leeks, chopped
2–3 garlic cloves, peeled and left whole
2 bay leaves
3 whole cloves
knob/pat of butter, for the sauce
salt and freshly ground black pepper

FRUIT PURÉE
500 g/1 lb 2 oz. russet apples and plums, peeled and cut into wedges (total weight)
250 ml/1 cup Rioja crianza red wine
2 tablespoons granulated white sugar
30 g/2 tablespoons butter
thumb-sized strip of orange peel

TO SERVE
large handful of watercress

SERVES 6–8

Cordero al chilindrón de toda la vida
SLOW-COOKED LAMB STEW

Chilindrón is the name of either a dish or a sauce, which is seldom seen in restaurants nowadays. This is home cooking at its best – a family dish that lingers in the memory of those who, like me, grew up eating very traditional food at home. It is cooked in spring (with the new season lamb) in a number of regions of northern Spain, in Aragón, Rioja, Basque Country and Navarra. Very often ham is included in the dish, although I prefer it without. Some recipes call for fresh green and red (bell) peppers, but I learned to prepare it with dry choricero red peppers, which I now buy ready prepared in paste form – they add a rich and earthy flavour. I use my own homemade meat stock, but you can now find good-quality organic stock cubes in supermarkets.

1.2 kg/2¾ lb. leg of lamb, deboned, trimmed and cut into chunks
Spanish extra virgin olive oil
4 garlic cloves (2 peeled and left whole and 2 peeled and chopped)
1½ large onions, peeled and chopped
150 ml/⅔ cup dry white wine
50 ml/scant ¼ cup meat stock (see page 10) or water
200 g/7 oz. fresh tomatoes, peeled and chopped
1 tablespoon red pepper paste
salt and freshly ground black pepper

TO SERVE
1 tablespoon chopped flat-leaf parsley (optional)
hunks of good-quality bread

SERVES 6

Season the lamb with plenty of salt and black pepper. Heat a few tablespoons of oil in a large, deep frying pan/skillet. Sauté the whole garlic cloves until they take on a little colour, then remove from the pan and set aside.

Increase the heat to high, add the lamb and seal the meat until it takes on some colour. Do not turn the lamb too often as you don't want to stew the meat. Return the whole garlic cloves to the pan and cook for a further few minutes. Transfer the lamb and garlic to a plate, cover to keep warm and set aside.

In the same pan, sauté the onions over a moderate heat, stirring often and adding a little more oil, if needed. Once the onions are soft, add the chopped garlic and sauté until it takes on a little colour. Next, pour in the wine and cook until the liquid has reduced by half. By now, the onions will be very soft and full of flavour.

Stir in the red pepper paste and add the tomatoes. Return the lamb to the pan and cook for 15–20 minutes, stirring frequently. If needed, add the meat stock or water. Bring everything to a simmer and cook for a further 30 minutes until the lamb is very tender and the sauce has reduced.

Scatter the parsley over the lamb, if using, then serve with hunks of good bread on the side to mop up the juices.

Pastelón de morcilla con piñones, sultanas y pera

BLACK PUDDING PIE WITH PINE NUTS, SULTANAS & PEARS

Basques love morcilla, a traditional black pudding/blood sausage, which is cooked all over Spain. Made with different ingredients, it's prepared in ways that vary from locality to locality. Morcilla can be eaten in a number of ways – on its own, shallow fried, added to a stew, in a pintxo or part of a celebratory dish such as this pastelón. I am not sure when I ate this dish for the first time, but it was probably at home in Spain. For me, this is a perfect dish to start a dinner party.

butter, for greasing

flour, for dusting

2 tablespoons Spanish extra virgin olive oil

1 small onion, peeled and thinly sliced

350 g/12½ oz. morcilla (black pudding/blood sausage)

1 tablespoon sultanas/golden raisins, soaked overnight in Oloroso sherry

2 tablespoons pine nuts, gently toasted

1 juicy pear or large apple, peeled and cut into small pieces

2 large/US extra-large eggs

300 g/10½ oz. block of ready-made puff pastry (or use homemade rough puff pastry, see page 179)

salt and freshly ground black pepper

SERVES 6–8

Preheat the oven to 180°C/160°C fan/350°F/Gas 4. Grease a baking sheet with butter, then lightly dust it with flour.

Heat the oil in a frying pan/skillet over a medium heat. Add the onion and sauté until soft and lightly golden. Set aside.

Remove the skin from the black pudding/blood sausage and cut it into slices. Crumble these slices into a deep mixing bowl. Drain the sultanas/golden raisins and add them to the bowl along with the pine nuts, pear or apple, one of the eggs and the sautéed onions. Using a fork, mash everything together to a coarse texture. Season with salt and black pepper.

Roll out the pastry into a large, thin circle, about 5 mm/¼ inch thick, then carefully lift it onto the prepared baking sheet. (Don't worry if the pastry overhangs the edges of the baking sheet as it will later be folded inwards.) Spoon the black pudding mixture into the centre of the pastry, leaving a very wide border around the edge. Fold the pastry border inwards to cover the filling and form a pie crust, gathering it together to make pleats where the pastry overlaps. Leave a small area of the filling uncovered in the centre of the pie so that the pastry can breathe. Trim away any excess pastry.

Beat the second egg to make a glaze. Prick the top of the pastry all over with a wooden skewer, then generously brush the pastry with the beaten egg.

Bake the pie in the preheated oven for about 30 minutes, or until the pastry has turned a lovely golden colour. Serve warm.

Pierna de cordero asada rellena de anchoas y alcaparras

ROASTED SHOULDER OF LAMB STUFFED WITH ANCHOVIES & CAPERS

In the northern part of Navarra, as in many other parts of Euskal Herria, sheep feeding on fresh green grass are a common sight. In the Basque Country, traditionally young lamb is used in a number of recipes in the kitchens of renowned restaurants, as well as those of home cooks. This is a sophisticated dish where a clever combination of sweet lamb and salty Cantabrian anchovies works well together. Ask your butcher to butterfly the shoulder of lamb and give you some bones to add to the roasting tin.

Preheat the oven to 180°C/160°C fan/350°F/Gas 4.

Place the lamb bones in a roasting tin/sheet pan. Bake in the preheated oven for 1 hour, or until they take on a golden colour.

Meanwhile, make the stuffing. Combine the anchovies, capers, garlic and parsley in a small bowl.

Season the inside of the lamb with salt and black pepper, then spread over the stuffing mixture. Neatly roll up the lamb to enclose the stuffing. Using kitchen twine, tie up the lamb at regular intervals to secure.

Bring 150 ml/⅔ cups water to the boil in a saucepan. Add the rosemary, remove the pan from the heat and leave to infuse for about 10 minutes. Remove the rosemary. Set aside the water.

Once the bones are roasted, place the lamb shoulder on top and pour over the rosemary-infused water and wine. Cover with foil.

Roast the lamb in the preheated oven for 30 minutes, then remove the foil. Reduce the temperature to 165°C/140°C fan/325°F/Gas 3, return the lamb to the oven to cook for a further 1 hour, or until the meat is very tender. Once the meat is cooked, remove the lamb from the oven, cover with foil to keep warm and leave to rest.

Remove and discard the bones, leaving any meat juices behind in the roasting tin. Add a splash of water to the tin and place it over a medium-high heat. Deglaze the tin by scraping up any brown bits and stirring them into the juices to make a light sauce.

Thickly slice the lamb and serve with the sauce and mashed potatoes on the side.

500 g/1 lb 2 oz. lamb bones, for roasting
800 g/1¾ lb. upper half shoulder of lamb, butterflied (ask your butcher to do this for you)
1 rosemary sprig
150 ml/⅔ cup dry white wine
salt and freshly ground black pepper

STUFFING
4–5 Cantabrian anchovies in olive oil
20 capers, drained and rinsed
2 garlic cloves, peeled and thinly sliced
15 g/½ oz. flat-leaf parsley, roughly chopped

TO SERVE
mashed potatoes

SERVES 4

Pechuga de pato con naranja sanguina, mermelada de naranja y brandy de Jerez

DUCK WITH BLOOD ORANGE, MARMALADE & BRANDY DE JEREZ

Ducks – and duck breasts in particular – are highly regarded in Basque kitchens. Some dishes cooked with duck are still influenced by La Alta Cocina Francesa (French haute cuisine), while other dishes are now being cooked in a lighter way. As good-value farmed ducks are now widely available, you have two options: to buy just the breasts or to buy a whole bird and ask the butcher to separate the breasts and legs, preparing the breasts so they are ready to cook. I prefer to buy a whole duck so I can make stock from the carcass and neck, then I freeze the legs and wings to prepare another dish.

As blood oranges are available only during a very short season, this dish can be prepared with other types of oranges, though preferably those from the Spanish Levante or Andalucía.

2 duck breasts
salt and freshly ground black pepper
1 blood orange, segmented, to serve

ORANGE SAUCE
thumb-sized strip of orange peel
a piece of lemon peel, cut into thin strips
25 g/1 oz. caster/superfine sugar
juice of 2 oranges
juice of ½ lemon
1½ tablespoons sherry vinegar
1 teaspoon brandy de Jerez
1 teaspoon orange liqueur
100 ml/scant ½ cup duck or chicken
    stock (see page 10), warmed
1 teaspoon orange marmalade
1 teaspoon cornflour/cornstarch or
    arrowroot, dissolved in a little water
salt and freshly ground black pepper

SERVES 2

First, prepare the sauce. In a small saucepan, bring 100ml/scant ½ cup water to the boil. Add the orange and lemon peel, reduce the heat and simmer for 2–3 minutes or until tender. Strain, reserving the peel. Set aside.

In a separate saucepan, dissolve the sugar in 50 ml/scant ¼ cup water. Bring to a fast boil, reducing the liquid to a light syrup. Carefully stir the orange and lemon juices into the syrup. Let the sauce reduce a little further and then stir in the sherry vinegar, brandy and orange liqueur.

Warm the stock, then stir in the marmalade until dissolved. Add this stock to the pan with the sauce and cook for a few minutes until all the flavours have mingled. Let it reduce a little more, then add the reserved orange and lemon peel. If the sauce is too thin, add the cornflour/cornstarch paste to thicken. Taste and adjust the seasoning, if needed. Set aside in the pan.

Using a very sharp knife, score the skin of the duck breasts, cutting in two directions to make a diamond-shaped pattern on the surface without slicing into the meat. Season with salt and black pepper.

Place the duck breasts, skin side down, in a cold frying pan/skillet. Place over a medium heat and cook for 12 minutes – as the pan warms, the skin will release its tasty fat and become crispy. Turn over the duck breasts and cook on the other side for a further 3 minutes (slightly longer if you prefer them less pink). Transfer the duck breasts to a plate, cover to keep warm and leave to rest for 10 minutes; this is important.

When ready to serve, slice the duck breasts, but not too thinly. Warm a serving dish under a hot tap and reheat the sauce. Arrange the sliced duck on the warm serving dish and cover with the hot sauce. Decorate the duck with some of the strips of peel and orange segments.

Pollo a la Vasca or Poulet Basquaise
FRENCH BASQUE CHICKEN CASSEROLE

This is a very popular recipe from Basque France. It clearly demonstrates the passion Basques share for all kinds of peppers, and above all, one rather special one: piment d'Espelette (espelette pepper). From the French commune of the same name in the Pyrénées-Atlantiques, piment d'Espelette really makes all the difference to this very tasty dish. It is a dried hot red chilli/chile pepper with an interesting piquancy that is quite unique. If you can't find espelette pepper, it can be substituted by cayenne pepper.

Season the chicken pieces with the piment d'Espelette or cayenne pepper, salt and black pepper.

Heat the olive oil in a large, cast-iron casserole dish/Dutch oven with a tight-fitting lid. When hot, add the butter and let it melt. Place the chicken pieces, skin-side down, in the pan and leave them to brown on one side. Do not turn the chicken over. Transfer the chicken to a plate, cover to keep warm and set aside.

Using the same pot, gently sauté the onion until soft. Add the Romano red peppers and green (bell) peppers to the pot, then cook together with the onion until tender.

Return the chicken pieces to the pot. Pour in the canned tomatoes and cook, stirring occasionally, until the liquid has reduced by half. Add the wine, stirring and scraping the bottom of the pot, and let the liquid reduce by half again. By now, the chicken will be becoming a little tender. Finally, pour in the chicken bouillon or stock, cover the pot with the lid and cook over a medium heat for a further 25–30 minutes, or until the chicken is completely tender.

When ready, garnish with the chopped parsley and serve with either steamed white rice or mashed potato on the side, as you prefer.

1 large whole chicken, cut into 8 pieces, with the skin left on
pinch of piment d'Espelette (espelette pepper) or cayenne pepper
2 tablespoons Spanish extra virgin olive oil
1 tablespoon butter
1 large onion, peeled and thinly sliced
2 fresh Romano red peppers, deseeded and chopped
2 green (bell) peppers, deseeded and chopped
1 x 400-g/14-oz can finely chopped plum tomatoes
75 ml/⅓ cup dry white wine
75 ml/⅓ cup chicken bouillon or chicken stock (see page 10)
salt and freshly ground black pepper

TO SERVE
handful of flat-leaf parsley, roughly chopped
steamed white rice or mashed potatoes

SERVES 4

Panceta al vino tinto con patatas

PORK BELLY COOKED IN RED WINE WITH PEPPERS & POTATOES

*Another recipe to impress the family or a group of friends.
A winter casserole full of flavour that would have been
prepared in a Basque gastronomic society, or perhaps by
a traditional home cook with plenty of time on their hands.*

Heat a couple of tablespoons of olive oil in a large, cast-iron
casserole dish/Dutch oven with a tight-fitting lid. Place the pieces
of pork in a single layer over the base of the pot, if possible. Add a
second layer of pork on top only if needed. Leave the meat to brown
all over, but turning it as few times as possible. Once browned,
season the pork with a little salt and black pepper. Do not over
season the meat. Transfer the pork pieces to a plate, cover to keep
warm and set aside. Empty the pork fat from the pot, reserving it
to be used later in another recipe.

Using the same pot, gently sauté the onions in 3 tablespoons of
fresh olive oil until soft. Add the garlic and cook for just 1 minute,
making sure it does not catch and burn. Add the chopped carrots,
celery and (bell) peppers, then cook until tender.

Return the pork pieces to the pot and cook, stirring, for a further
minute. Pour in the red wine, bring to the boil and cook for about
10–12 minutes. Add the stock, bring back to the boil, then reduce
the heat to low and simmer everything for 1 hour.

Add the potatoes and gently cook over a low heat until tender.
Once tender, remove a few potatoes to a dish or plate, mash with
a fork and return them to the pot. Shake the pot.

When ready, garnish with the chopped parsley and drizzle with
some extra virgin olive oil. Serve with hunks of bread on the side
and a glass of red wine from the Rioja Alavesa region, if you like.

Spanish olive oil, for frying
750 g/1 lb 10 oz. pork belly, cut into
    small pieces
150 g/5½ oz. cebolletas (or large spring
    onions/scallions), peeled and finely
    chopped
5 garlic cloves, peeled and finely
    chopped
100 g/3½ oz. carrots, peeled and
    finely chopped
50 g/1¾ oz. celery sticks/ribs,
    finely chopped
50 g/1¾ oz. red (bell) peppers,
    deseeded and finely chopped
750 ml/3 cups Spanish red wine
1.5 litres/1.5 quarts chicken stock
    or meat stock (see page 10)
600 g/1 lb. 5 oz. potatoes, peeled
    and cut into small cubes
salt and freshly ground black pepper

TO SERVE
handful of flat-leaf parsley, roughly
    chopped
Spanish extra virgin olive oil
hunks of good-quality bread
glasses of Rioja red wine (optional)

SERVES 6

Chuleta a la parrilla con piquillos confitados
CHARCOAL-GRILLED T-BONE STEAK WITH CONFIT PIQUILLO PEPPERS

In the Basque Country, parrillero and parrillera are the men and women in charge of the grill. They are professionals working in asadores (restaurants that specialise in grilling meat or fish), as well as sidreras (cider houses). In such places, I have eaten superb chuleta (T-bone steak) grilled to perfection over hot coals.

You can cook a perfect chuleta on your own barbecue, as long as you follow my directions to the letter. The best steaks come from cows that are 6 or 7 years old and should be 5 cm/ 2 inches thick, cut in a perpendicular way to ensure the same thickness at both ends. Once grilled and rested, cut the meat into thick slices and serve with potatoes, salad and roasted piquillo peppers. I wrap a couple of potatoes in foil, bake them in the embers, then serve these with a little sea salt and extra virgin olive oil.

1 x 230-g/8-oz. can or jar of whole
    chargrilled piquillo peppers
Spanish extra virgin olive oil
1 x 1-kg/2¼-lb. T-bone steak
coarse sea salt, to taste

TO SERVE
baked potatoes (see introduction)
crisp green salad

SERVES 2

First, prepare the confit piquillo peppers. Drain the peppers from the can or jar, reserving the liquid. Brush a large, shallow frying pan/skillet with olive oil and place over a medium heat. Add the piquillo peppers to the pan in a single layer, if possible, and fry for 2–3 minutes or until they take on some colour, turning them once.

Transfer the peppers to a saucepan, again in a single layer, pour in enough olive oil to cover and confit for a couple of hours over a very low heat. Remove the peppers from the pan, then pour a little of the reserved liquid from the can or jar into the oil. Set aside.

Well in advance of serving, light the barbecue using plenty of charcoal. Once the charcoal has turned white, place the grill about 15 cm/6 inches above the heat.

Generously sprinkle the steak with sea salt. (The meat will absorb as much salt as it needs during grilling.) Make a cut across the edge fat to allow it to contract during cooking without distorting the meat.

Place the steak on the grill and cook over the hot coals for 8–10 minutes – you must avoid or at least control any flames so do not leave the barbecue even for a second. Move the grill up to 30 cm/12 inches above the heat. Turn over the steak, sprinkle more salt on top and cook for a further 10 minutes. The meat should be well caramelised, with a dark colour on the exterior and pink in the centre. The steak should never be served raw.

Using a clean cloth, brush away any salt not absorbed by the meat. Rest the steak before serving with the confit piquillo peppers, baked potatoes and green salad.

Lomo de cerdo con leche

MILK-BRAISED PORK LOIN

This is another festive pork recipe, which is often included in traditional Basque cookbooks. I happily prepare it any time of the year. The sauce is quite unique; it is essential to keep an eye on it while cooking, controlling the temperature and stirring frequently so the meat does not stick to the bottom of the pan – you may need to add extra milk, if needed. The meat will become very tender and the sauce will take on the wonderful colour of café con leche (milky coffee). I serve mine with creamy mashed potatoes and green vegetables.

Heat the olive oil in a deep saucepan. Add the pork and seal the meat until it takes on some colour. Add the garlic cloves to the pan and cook for a further minute. Remove and discard the garlic.

Pour in enough milk to cover the pork, then add the bay leaves and sprinkle in the white pepper and salt. Bring the milk to the boil, then reduce the heat to low and simmer, stirring frequently, for about 45 minutes or until the milk has reduced to a very creamy texture and turned darker in colour. Do not overcook the milk sauce or the milk solids and liquid will split, looking rather like ricotta.

When ready, cut the pork into thick slices and serve either hot or cold on buttery mashed potatoes or steamed white rice, and smothered in the creamy sauce. Serve some grilled or steamed green vegetables alongside, if you like.

2 tablespoons Spanish extra virgin olive oil
1.2 kg/2¾ lb. boneless pork loin, in one piece
2 garlic cloves, peeled and left whole
full-fat/whole milk (enough to cover the pork)
2 bay leaves (fresh or dried)
a pinch of ground white pepper
a pinch of salt

TO SERVE
buttery mashed potatoes or steamed white rice
grilled or steamed green vegetables

SERVES 6

Sukalki de jarrete de ternera y guisantes
TRADITIONAL BEEF & VEGETABLE STEW WITH POTATOES

Meat stews never fall out of fashion in the Basque Country, and sukalki remains a very popular one. The word sukalki in the Basque language translates as 'kitchen', 'stove' or 'made on the stove'. Originally from Vizcaya, this dish is still celebrated today at popular events where professional and amateur cooks battle for supremacy in front of delighted onlookers, eager to taste the best dish of the day!

You need the right ingredients, a combination of good meat, vegetables and wine, but as ever, the secret to this dish is time and patience. When cooked with plenty of both, success is guaranteed. Served with plenty of bread, a crisp salad and good red wine, this is a great dinner-party dish

750 g/1 lb. 10 oz. beef shank (ask your
    butcher to debone), cut into chunks
plain/all-purpose flour, to coat the beef
Spanish extra virgin olive oil
2 shallots, peeled and finely diced
1 large red onion, peeled and finely diced
1 carrot, peeled and finely diced
1 large leek (white part only), finely sliced
2 garlic cloves, peeled and finely chopped
250 ml/1 cup txakoli white wine
2 tablespoons red pepper paste
3 tablespoons tomato sauce (see page
    93), or use a good quality jarred sauce
100 g/3½ oz. fresh tomatoes
meat or chicken stock (see page 10),
    as needed
2 potatoes, peeled, quartered and
    placed in a bowl of cold water
150 g/1 cup fresh or frozen peas
salt and freshly ground black pepper
handful of flat-leaf parsley, finely
    chopped, to garnish

SERVES 4

Season the beef with plenty of salt and black pepper, then lightly coat the meat in flour. Heat a few tablespoons of olive oil in a large casserole dish/Dutch oven. Add the beef to the pan and seal the meat until it takes on some colour. Do not turn the beef too often as you do not want to stew the meat. Transfer the beef to a plate, cover to keep warm and set aside.

Remove some of the excess oil from the pan, then add the finely chopped shallots, onion, carrot, leek and garlic. Gently sauté the vegetables to release their liquids until very soft and flavourful – this will take time.

Pour the wine into the pan and cook until the alcohol has totally evaporated and the liquid reduced. Stir in the red pepper paste and tomato sauce. Using the large holes of a box grater, grate in the fresh tomatoes, discarding the skins. Return the beef to the pan, stir briefly and cover with the stock. Reduce the heat to low and very gently cook for at least 3 hours.

When the beef is very tender, drain the potatoes and dry them on a clean dish towel or paper towels. Fry the potatoes in plenty of olive oil in a deep frying pan/skillet. Once they are almost cooked, remove the potatoes from the oil. (This is important as they will finish cooking in the stew.) Set aside and keep warm.

Using a slotted spoon, remove the meat from the sauce and set aside. The sauce should still be quite liquid. Skim off any excess oil from the surface of the sauce, then place it in a blender and blitz until smooth. Strain the sauce through a fine-mesh sieve/strainer and return to the pan, before reintroducing the beef. Cook for a further few minutes to warm through, then add the fried potatoes and peas. Taste and adjust the seasoning, if needed. Cook for a final 10–15 minutes for all the flavours to mingle.

Scatter the parsley over the stew just before serving.

Cocornices en salsa de manzana, verduras, txakoli y sidra

QUAILS IN AN APPLE CIDER SAUCE

Recipes with game birds are very popular in the whole of the Basque Country. Many are modern recipes prepared by some of the top chefs, other have always been cooked at local restaurants and of course at home. This recipe originally came from a sidrería (cider house) and includes both cider and the local wine txakoli with delicious results.

Season the quails with plenty of salt and black pepper, then lightly dust with flour. Heat the olive oil in a large saucepan or cast-iron casserole dish/Dutch oven. Add the quails to the pan and seal the birds until they take on some colour. Turn the quails to brown them all over. Set aside in the pan.

Next, make the sauce. Heat the olive oil in a large deep frying pan/skillet. Add the onion and sauté until soft. Add the apples, carrots and leeks, then pour in the wine and cider. Cook until all the fruit and vegetables are tender and the liquid has reduced by half.

Finally, add the chicken stock and cook, stirring continuously, until all the sauce ingredients are fully incorporated. Transfer the quails to a serving dish or platter, then pass the sauce though a fine-mesh sieve/strainer.

Serve the quails with the sauce spooned over the top, accompanied by cubes of fried bread to mop up the sauce. This is a perfect recipe to enjoy with Basque cider.

6 quails, cleaned and dressed
100 ml/scant ½ cup Spanish extra
   virgin olive oil
plain/all-purpose flour, for coating
salt and freshly ground black pepper
cubes of fried bread, to serve

SAUCE
2 tablespoons olive oil
1 large onion, chopped
2 apples, peeled and quartered
3 carrots, peeled and chopped
2 leeks (white part only), chopped
75 ml/⅓ cup txakoli white wine
   (or any dry white wine)
75 ml/⅓ cup cider
75 ml/⅓ cup chicken stock (see page 10)

SERVES 6

THE SWEET TASTE OF THE BASQUES

Indulgent desserts & cakes

Basque desserts:
A passion for sugar

Every year, at the end of summer, we sail to Bilbao on the long journey to our house in Andalucía. As we take the car ferry, we reach the Basque Country after two days in early morning. That is just in time for breakfast in Santurce, close to the port of Bilbao, before heading south towards Old Castile and on toward our destination further south. At a café in Santurce, we have coffee served in an old Spanish way, in a glass accompanied by one or two *pasteles de Bilbao*, still warm, which are made with a crunchy pastry and the popular *crema pastelera* (crème pâtissière/pastry cream). There are many other treats, sweet or savoury, we could choose, but we love the *pasteles*.

On the subject of Basque sweet things, and making a list of the most original as well as the most common examples to be found today, I thought to blend as, in a recipe, some local food history and what I found while travelling in Euskal Herria. I started my list three decades ago in north-west Navarra, between the villages of Erratzu in the Baztan valley and the elegant Bera de Bidasoa. I was looking for early recipes that had managed to reach modernity but keep their authenticity. In the picturesque Erratzo, I found the best *Mamia* I have ever tasted. It is also called *gaztambera* or simply *cuajada*. This is a curd of great texture made with ewe's milk and has a slightly burnt flavour (see page 176). In Bera, I managed to organise a short meeting with the late Julio Caro Baroja, the great historian, anthropologist and specialist in Basque culture. While talking to him, it became clear that he was partial to an ancient sweet soup with an intriguing Basque name, *inzaursalsa*, which is made with walnuts. It is still made at Christmas time. After the journey I thought that perhaps I would eventually find other similar preparations, but so far I have failed. Compared with the sweet kitchens in other parts of Spain, which have been enriched by foreign food cultures during the Middle Ages, Basque early recipes, as delicious as they are, are fewer in number and ingredients, affected by geography and climate. During the Middle Ages, independent-spirited Basques fought for freedom instead of for kitchen sophistication, missing out on some of rich legacy left behind by the Islamic invasion of the Iberian Peninsula, for example.

What can be seen, however, is the sweet kitchen sophistication brought by French pâtissiers moving south after the French Revolution. They were looking for work which they found in towns and cities, particularly in the elegant San Sebastián. Today with Spanish or Basque names and some local adaptation, pâtisseries and restaurants include on their menus such things as *tejas*, almond *pantxineta* and the *pastel Vasco* (Basque gâteau) among other examples from a rich French heritage not to be forgotten.

In a separate group, I have to mention recipes from *la pastelería alavesa* (from the province of Alava), sweet and old-fashioned recipes reflecting the sweet tooth of the *alaveses*. In this book you can find a recipe for *goxua*, a local speciality from the city of Vitoria-Gasteiz. The *pastel de Sarah* with lots of butter and almonds is also one of the best.

Apart from these, there are a number of very popular recipes to be found in home kitchens and more traditional restaurants. These are not necessarily original Basque recipes as they are enjoyed in other parts of Spain. Recipes such as the *torrijas*, for example, made with bread, milk, sugar and eggs or the *flan de caramelo* with eggs, milk and caramel. The *tocino de cielo* is similar to the flan, however it is steamed and does not contain milk. It is prepared with a sugar syrup, egg yolks and caramel. The *leche frita* (fried milk), which may sound boring but is equally delicious, is made with flour, milk and

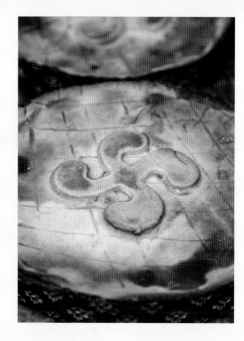

sugar and then fried with beaten egg. It is another of the favourite ones.

Many of the recipes included in my list, have now been adopted by Basque chefs who, since the late 1970s, started bringing dishes up to date and most importantly creating innovative and irresistible new puddings and desserts. In the majority of cases, innovative recipes are not that easy to make in home kitchens but I have not been able to resist describing a couple of preparations from chefs I admire that can be made at home.

Clockwise from top left: Café Iruña, Bilbao; pastel Vasco, a popular traditional dessert; fresh walnuts for sale at the market in Pamplona, Navarra; slices of Basque burnt cheesecake on display; an array of sweet bakes. Overleaf: trees heavy with lemons.

Tarta de queso de La Viña en San Sebastián
BAKED CHEESECAKE FROM LA VIÑA IN SAN SEBASTIÁN

It is easy to understand why this Basque baked cheesecake has become so popular, admired throughout the whole of Spain and, indeed, across the rest of the world. It has an unusual caramelised – almost burnt – exterior with the creamiest, silkiest interior. It was created in 1990 by Santiago Rivera, chef patron of La Viña in the heart of the Basque city of San Sebastián. This cheesecake rapidly became known as 'the jewel in the Spanish sweet crown'. For me, it is certainly one of the jewels, as there are many.

570 g/1¼ lb. cream cheese
  (such as Philadelphia)
4 large/US extra-large eggs
230 g/1 cup plus 2 tablespoons
  caster/superfine sugar
1 teaspoon vanilla extract
10 g/2 teaspoons plain/all-purpose
  flour, sifted
285 ml/1 cup plus 2 tablespoons
  double/heavy cream

*deep 18-cm/7-inch springform cake
  tin/pan with removable base*

SERVES 6–8

Preheat the oven to 200°C/180°C fan/400°F/Gas 6.

Tear off a sheet of parchment paper that is large enough to line the entire cake tin/pan and generously extend well over the top edge. Dampen with water to soften the paper and then, using both hands, ring out as much of the water as possible. Line the cake tin with the paper.

Put the cream cheese into a deep mixing bowl. Using an electric hand mixer, slowly incorporate the eggs, one by one. Add the sugar and vanilla extract, then whisk again. Do the same with the flour. Once all these ingredients are well blended, gradually add the cream until fully incorporated.

Pour the cheesecake mixture into the lined cake tin. Bake in the preheated oven for about 45 minutes or until the top looks almost burnt, but the inside is just set. Leave to cool completely, then remove from the cake tin and peel away the parchment paper before slicing and serving.

Torrija con manzana caramelizada y guirlache de piñones
BREAD PUDDING WITH CARAMELISED APPLES & PINE NUT BRITTLE

Bread puddings are very popular in the Basque Country, and torrijas is one of them. It is similar to French toast, although there are some clear differences between the two. Torrijas are made from slices of bread dipped in a mixture of milk, egg and sugar, which are then coated in more egg and fried in olive oil. They are served sprinkled with sugar and ground cinnamon. In Andalucía, torrijas are often dipped in wine instead of milk and coated in a sugar syrup.

Torrijas were, and still are, prepared during Easter for a mid-morning or afternoon treat. In the last few years, they have appeared on menus in assorted shapes and made with all kinds of ingredients. Here, I prepare torrijas in a very different way using only the crusts of an artisan white loaf, served with caramelised apples and guirlache (pine nut brittle).

TORRIJAS
250 g/9 oz. crusts of an artisan white loaf
3 large/US extra-large egg yolks
50 g/¼ cup caster/superfine sugar
500 ml/2 cups full-fat/whole milk
150 ml/⅔ cup single/light cream
1 cinnamon stick
seeds scraped from ½ vanilla pod/bean
vegetable oil or light olive oil, for frying
2 beaten eggs, for coating

PINE NUT BRITTLE
100 g/½ cup caster/superfine sugar
40 g/⅓ cup pine nuts

CARAMELISED APPLES
60 g/¼ cup/½ stick unsalted butter
2–3 Granny Smith apples, left unpeeled, cored and cut into wedges
100 g/½ cup demerara/raw sugar

TO SERVE
vanilla ice cream

SERVES 6

The day before, remove the crusts from the loaf and tear into small pieces. Leave them uncovered to dry out.

To make the torrijas, whisk the egg yolks with the sugar, milk and cream in a large saucepan. Add the cinnamon stick and vanilla seeds, then warm it over a low heat. Remove the pan from the heat and leave to cool, letting the spices infuse the mixture.

Place the dried-out bread in a dish. Remove and discard the cinnamon stick from the milk mixture, then pour it over the bread. Leave to soak for at least 2 hours.

Meanwhile, prepare the pine nut brittle. Dissolve the sugar in 100 ml/scant ½ cup water in a saucepan. Place the pan over a high heat and cook until it turns into an amber-coloured caramel – this takes about 5 minutes. Add the pine nuts and stir well with a wooden spoon to coat all the nuts in the caramel. Remove the pan from the heat and immediately tip out the mixture onto a heatproof surface (I use a marble slab brushed with oil). Using a palette knife, swiftly spread the mixture thinly over the surface before it hardens. Remove the brittle from the surface and break into irregular shards.

To caramelise the apples, melt the butter in a heavy-based pan over a medium heat. Add the apple wedges, sprinkle over the sugar and cook until tender and lightly golden. Leave to cool.

Once soaked, strain the bread through a fine-mesh sieve/strainer to remove the excess liquid. Using your hands, squeeze out any remaining moisture. Divide the soaked bread into 6 equal portions. Using your hands, shape each portion into a ball and then flatten slightly into a round.

In a frying pan/skillet, heat 5 cm/2 inches of oil. When hot, coat each torrija in the beaten egg and fry until lightly golden. Remove from the pan and transfer to paper towels to absorb any excess oil. Serve warm with the caramelised apples, a few shards of the pine nut brittle and a scoop of vanilla ice cream.

Merenguitos con helado de vainilla y salsa templada de frambuesas

MINI MERINGUES WITH VANILLA ICE CREAM & WARM RASPBERRY SAUCE

I don't remember when I first tasted raspberries but I know it was in England and it still brings a smile to my face. Before that, I had eaten plenty of strawberries in Spain, including wonderful fresitas (wild strawberries) that my father brought home from time to time, but no raspberries. Now raspberries are available throughout Spain at a reasonable price. Some of my friends even grow raspberries themselves in the Basque Country.

Not so long ago, I saw a dessert similar to this one at a modern Basque restaurant. It was my first taste of a warm raspberry sauce and I was impressed. If you prefer, you can buy ready-made ice cream; there are some very good brands on the market.

VANILLA ICE CREAM
2 vanilla pods/beans
500 ml/2 cups full-fat/whole milk
500 ml/2 cups double/heavy cream
150 g/¾ cup caster/superfine sugar
4 large/US extra-large egg yolks
(reserve the egg whites for the meringues, see below)

MINI MERINGUES
3 large/US extra-large egg whites
150 g/¾ cup caster/superfine sugar
pinch of salt

RASPBERRY SAUCE
350 g/3 cups raspberries

ice-cream machine (optional)

SERVES 8

To make the ice cream, place the milk, cream and 100 g/½ cup of the sugar in a saucepan. Using a sharp knife, split the vanilla pods lengthways and scrape the seeds into the pan, then add the pods too. Warm the milk mixture, stirring, over a low heat for a few minutes.

In a mixing bowl, beat the egg yolks with the remaining sugar. Add 2–3 tablespoons of the warm milk to the egg mixture and stir until smooth. Next, pour the egg mixture into the saucepan with the milk. Stirring with a wooden spoon, warm over a medium heat until it thickens slightly to make a custard. Cover the pan and chill for about 15 minutes, then let the mixture cool completely. Transfer the mixture to an ice-cream machine and churn following the instructions.

If you don't have an ice-cream maker, simply place the ice-cream mixture in a freezerproof container with a lid and freeze for 2–3 hours. Remove the container from the freezer and stir the mixture once or twice during freezing time to break up any crystals.

Next, prepare the meringues. Using an electric whisk, beat the egg whites in a grease-free bowl until soft peaks form. Continue whisking while gradually adding the sugar with the salt until the perfect meringue forms.

Preheat the oven to 150°C/130°C fan/300°F/Gas 2. Line a large baking sheet with parchment paper. Heap spoonfuls of the meringue mixture onto the lined baking sheet. Bake in the preheated oven for about 20 minutes or until crisp. Leaving the oven door slightly ajar, let the meringues cool down. Remove the meringues from the oven and set aside.

Place the raspberries in a saucepan and gently warm over a medium heat, mashing the fruit into a coarse sauce. Keep warm.

When ready to serve, place two or three mini meringues on each plate with a scoop of vanilla ice cream, then drizzle over the warm raspberry sauce.

Copa de arroz con leche con infusion de limón
LEMONY RICE PUDDING

This recipe is a celebration of the lemon trees found all along the Cantabrian coast in northern Spain. It is also an homage to the Basque restaurant, Zuberoa, admired by chefs as well as the thousands of people prepared to travel to eat something really special.

For many years, I could not visit the region without making a reservation at Zuberoa, just outside the city of San Sebastián. For many of us, it was one of the best restaurants in Spain. The reason was simple: the divine dishes on offer were based on la cocina vasca de siempre (the food of the mother and grandmother).

At Zuberoa, dishes were made elegant yet remained gustosa (tasty). They were brought into the world of contemporary Basque food without fuss and without losing any of the characteristics of the cooking loved by all Basques: authentic, delicious and brought beautifully up to date.

In 2023, sadly Zuberoa closed its doors permanently. Thankfully I had the privilege of sitting for a few hours at one of the restaurant tables, enjoying every second and admiring the talented chefs in the kitchen. My memories of dining there will never leave me and I will continue to try to cook recipes inspired by that truly great restaurant.

1.2 litres/5 cups full-fat/whole milk
2 pieces of lemon zest
1 cinnamon stick
175 g/1 cup Calasparra rice (short-grain Spanish paella rice) or Arborio
175 g/scant 1 cup caster/superfine sugar
grated lemon and lime zest, to decorate

LEMON SYRUP
2 strips of lemon zest
75 g/⅓ cup caster/superfine sugar
juice of 3 lemons

SERVES 6

Place the milk, lemon zest and cinnamon stick in a saucepan and bring to the boil over a high heat. Reduce the heat to low and leave the milk to infuse for at least 15 minutes. Remove and discard the lemon zest and cinnamon stick.

Bring the milk back to the boil and add the rice. Reduce the heat to low and gently cook, stirring continuously, for 30 minutes. Add the sugar and cook, while stirring, for a further 15 minutes. If the rice pudding is too thick, add more hot milk and stir again.

Once the rice is tender, pass it through a sieve/strainer to separate the rice pudding from the milk, leaving the rice fairly moist. Set aside in a cool place.

To make the lemon syrup, blanch the zest in boiling water. Remove the zest and set aside. In a separate saucepan, dissolve the sugar in 150 ml/⅔ cup water. Bring to the boil until it begins to thicken into a syrup. Remove the pan from the heat, add the blanched lemon zest to the syrup. Leave the syrup to cool before adding the lemon juice. Remove the zest and set aside.

To serve, spoon the rice pudding into each Martini glass. Add a thin layer of the lemon syrup, then pour over some of the thickened rice milk. Finally, decorate each glass with some grated lemon and lime zest.

Mamia de leche de oveja con jarabe de arce y frutillas
BASQUE MILK PUDDING WITH MAPLE SYRUP & FIGS

During the making of the BBC television series, Spain on a Plate, *we visited Errazu, a small Basque-Navarrese locality near the border with France. In Errazu we filmed the making of mamia, also known as cuajada. A popular dessert made with sheep's milk, it is one of the oldest desserts made in the Basque Country.*

When made in the traditional way, mamia is cooked in a kaiku – an ancient wooden pitcher that was used to carry grain and for milking animals. Eventually the kaiku was used to make mamia following this method: stones from a riverbed were heated in the red hot embers of a cooking stove and placed in the bottom of the kaiku. A spoonful of sugar was then added; on contact with the hot stones, the sugar would ignite for a few seconds. After this milk was added and left to take on a slightly burnt flavour, which is characteristic of this dessert... and delicious. The milk was left to cool to 37°C/98°F before a few drops of natural rennet were added. This was blended with the milk, which was then allowed to curdle. Today the method for making mamia is somewhat easier, although when made in a wooden kaiku the creaminess and flavour of this dessert is quite unique.

I recommend preparing this dessert on the day of serving, and to serve it at room temperature. Sheep's milk has a higher fat content than cow's or goat's, which makes mamia very creamy. The addition of a little salt brings out the best flavours of the milk, making it truly delectable. When preparing mamia, you can use a vegetarian rennet, if preferred.

1 tablespoon caster/superfine sugar
500 ml/2 cups sheep's milk
few drops of rennet
pinch of salt
maple syrup or honey, to serve
fresh figs or summer berries, to serve

SERVES 4

In a small saucepan, dissolve the sugar in the milk over a medium heat. Using a kitchen thermometer to check the temperature, heat the milk to 37°C/98°F.

Add the rennet to the pan, then gently stir in one direction only using a wooden spoon. Stir in the salt and leave the milk to cool and curdle.

Once ready, divide the milk pudding equally between individual bowls. Drizzle over some maple syrup or honey and top with some halved fresh figs or a handful of summer berries.

Intxaursaltsa
WALNUT CREAM

Intxaursaltsa is a type of nut cream prepared in the Basque Country to celebrate Nochebuena (Christmas Eve). It is also a celebration of the walnut itself and the attractive walnut trees often seen in the Basque countryside. The ancient recipe for intxaursaltsa is older than the recipe for turrón (nougat), another classic Spanish festive sweet treat, although they are very different preparations.

Originally intxaursaltsa was made with water instead of milk and very little sugar or no sugar at all. Although it has evolved to please the modern palate, it has retained a strong attachment to Basque food history.

300 g/3 cups (shelled weight) walnuts, shelled, plus extra to decorate
1 cinnamon stick
1 litre/4 cups full-fat/whole milk
100 g/½ cup caster/granulated sugar
pinch of salt
maple syrup or honey, to serve

SERVES 6

Blanch the walnuts in a saucepan of boiling water to remove any bitterness. Drain the walnuts, then wrap them in a thick, clean cloth and crush them with a mallet to form a thick paste.

Bring 1 litre/4 cups water to the boil in a saucepan. Add the cinnamon stick and walnut paste. Reduce the heat and gently simmer, stirring continuously, until almost all the liquid has evaporated. Remove the cinnamon stick. Add the milk and sugar, then gently simmer again, while stirring, for a further 30–40 minutes or until the mixture thickens to a light cream.

When ready, divide the walnut cream equally between individual bowls. Drizzle with maple syrup or honey and top with walnut halves. Serve warm.

Masa de hojaldre
ROUGH PUFF PASTRY

Basques love puff pastry. They use it to make cakes, desserts and even pintxos. Following the suggestion of a friend, who is an amazing pastry maker, I use a grater when adding the butter.

240 g/1 cup/2¼ sticks very cold butter
240 g/1¾ cups plain/all-purpose flour, plus extra for dusting
½ teaspoon salt
1 tablespoon granulated white sugar
a few tablespoons ice-cold water

SERVES 6

To get the butter very cold, place it in the freezer for 10–12 minutes. Combine the flour, salt and sugar in a large mixing bowl and stir together with a fork. Take the butter out of the freezer, then grate it into the flour mixture as quickly as possible and mix well with the fork. Add a few teaspoons of ice-cold water, little by little, working it into the flour mixture for a few seconds with your fingers into rough crumbs. First with your fingers and palm of one hand, and then both hands, work it into a rough dough and shape into a ball. If needed, add a little more water, but only enough to make it possible to handle the dough.

If your hands are warm, cool them down in ice-cold water. Tear off a piece of cling film/plastic wrap and lay it over a cold work surface. Place the dough on the cling film and, using your hands, flatten it into a neat square. Wrap the dough in the cling film and rest in the fridge for at least 20 minutes.

Remove the dough from the fridge, unwrap it and place on the cold work surface. Dust the surface and dough with flour. Roll the dough into a large rectangle. Fold down the top two-thirds and then the bottom third over the middle (like a business letter). Turn it 90 degrees, then roll and fold again. Do this three times. Re-wrap in cling film and chill in the fridge for at least 3 hours or until ready to use.

Pantxineta

PUFF PASTRY TART WITH ALMOND PASTRY CREAM

If I had to choose a dessert that immediately transports me to the Basque world of food, it would be pantxineta. Although it is probably of French origin, this classic tart has been associated with the pastelería (bakery), Casa Otaegui, in San Sebastián since 1915. Otaegui knew how to please the palates of their aristocratic clientele who lived in the city during the summer months.

Made with puff pastry, crema pastelera (crème pâtissière/pastry cream) and plenty of almonds, this tart can be very successfully cooked at home. The best pantxinetas use home-made pastry, but for convenience you can use any good quality, ready-made puff pastry.

2 sheets of ready-rolled puff pastry,
  5 mm/⅛ inch thick (or use homemade
  rough puff pastry, see page 179)
1 medium/US large egg, beaten, to glaze
25 g/¼ cup toasted chopped almonds
25 g/¼ cup untoasted chopped almonds
icing/confectioner's sugar
single/light cream, to serve (optional)

ALMOND PASTRY CREAM
750 ml/3 cups plus 3 tablespoons
  full-fat/whole milk
strip of lemon peel (with pith removed)
strip of orange peel (with pith removed)
1 small cinnamon stick
seeds from ½ vanilla pod/bean
2 large/US extra-large egg yolks
100 g/½ cup caster/superfine sugar
35 g/2 tablespoons cornflour/cornstarch
50 g/½ cup ground almonds
30 g/2 tablespoons butter

*25-cm/10-inch round tart tin/pan
  with removable base*

SERVES 6–8

First, prepare the almond pastry cream. In a saucepan, heat 600 ml/2½ cups of the milk. Remove the pan from the heat just before the milk starts to boil, then add the lemon and orange peel, cinnamon stick and vanilla seeds. Cover and leave to infuse for 15 minutes.

Using a metal whisk in a large bowl, beat the egg yolks and sugar together until pale and very creamy. Set aside.

In a small bowl, mix the cornflour/cornstarch with the remaining milk. Add to the large bowl with the egg yolks and sugar, then whisk again. Strain the infused milk into the bowl, discarding the peel and spices, then add the ground almonds and whisk again.

Return the mixture to the saucepan and heat, stirring continuously, until it starts to thicken. Reduce the heat. If it becomes too thick, add some more warm milk. Add the butter and continue stirring for a few minutes. Remove the pan from the heat, transfer the pastry cream to a clean bowl and cover with cling film/plastic wrap. Let cool before chilling in the fridge for 2 hours

Preheat the oven to 180°C/160°C fan/350°F/Gas 4.

Unroll the first pastry sheet, leaving it on its parchment paper. Using a rolling pin, gently flatten the edges. Place the tart tin/pan on the pastry and punch out a neat circle. Prick the pastry all over with a fork. Lift the pastry onto a baking sheet with the parchment paper still in place. Remove the pastry cream from the fridge. Using a spatula, spread it evenly over the pastry, leaving a 1.5-cm/½-inch border around the edge. Sprinkle the pastry cream with the toasted chopped almonds.

Using the second sheet, cut another circle of pastry to the same size as the first. Carefully place it on top of the pastry cream, pressing down with your fingers to seal the edges of the pastry. Brush the top of the pastry with the beaten egg and scatter over the untoasted chopped almonds and icing/confectioner's sugar.

Bake in the preheated oven for 35–40 minutes. Serve while slightly warm with a little cream, if you like.

Pasteles de arroz de Bilbao
'RICE CAKES' FROM BILBAO

Why is a small tart that does not contain any rice known in Bilbao as a pastel de arroz (rice cake). It is a bit of a puzzle to which, it seems, there is no easy answer. Is this a capricious oddity similar to the British mince pie or Welsh rabbit, I wondered as I started researching through old books and asking questions around the city? Did the idea arrive with Basque mariners, returning from the Far East? Perhaps from the Philippine islands (which were once in Spanish hands) or possibly from Japan, where rice cakes have always been in existence. Or was that all just speculation?

What I did find, however, was a fascinating early twentieth-century book entitled, El Amparo: sus platos clásicos, written by three sisters – Ursula, Sira and Filipa Azcaray Egileor. This opened up an avenue of research as they included a recipe for small cakes made with arroz con leche (rice pudding), enriched with egg yolks, butter and a little cinnamon. The sisters mentioned that pasteles de arroz could also be made with natillas, a light pastry cream typical of the city of Victoria in Alava. They can also be made with rice flour instead of wheat flour.

I like to buy freshly-made puff pastry from my local delicatessen that comes rolled up in paper. Of course, you can also buy ready-rolled pastry sheets from the store, or make your own rough puff pastry (see page 179), if you prefer.

2 sheets of ready-rolled puff pastry, 5 mm/⅛ inch thick (or use homemade rough puff pastry, see page 179)

FILLING
75 g/⅓ cup/¾ stick butter, at room temperature, plus extra for greasing
130 g/⅔ cup caster/superfine sugar
2 medium/US large eggs
125 g/1 cup plain/all-purpose flour
500 ml/2 cups plus 1 tablespoon full-fat/whole milk

12-hole bun tin/pan, 7 x 12 cm/ 3 x 5 inches

8-cm/3¼-inch round cookie cutter

MAKES 12

Preheat the oven to 180°C/160°C fan/350°F/Gas 4. Grease the moulds of the bun tin/pan with butter.

Unroll the pastry sheets, leaving them on their parchment paper. Lay another sheet of parchment paper on top, then gently flatten the pastry with a rolling pin. Using a cookie cutter, punch out 12 rounds slightly larger than the moulds of the bun tin. Place a pastry round in each mould. Prick the pastry all over with a fork. Fill each mould with a few ceramic baking beans or dried beans to stop the pastry lifting. Bake in the preheated oven for 10 minutes.

Meanwhile, prepare the filling. Using an electric hand mixer, beat the butter and sugar together in a bowl until pale and fluffy. Add the eggs, one by one, and mix until each one is fully incorporated before gradually adding the flour. Slowly add the milk, little by little. The mixture will appear to have curdled – don't worry, this is how it should look. Transfer the filling to a jug/pitcher.

Remove the bun tin from the oven and empty the baking beans from the pastry cases. Pour the filling mixture into each pastry case, right up to the rim. Bake in the centre of the preheated oven for 15–20 minutes or until golden. Serve either warm or cold.

Mi Goxua Alavés

MY HOMEMADE SWEET TREATS FROM ALAVA

Basques have a sweet tooth, especially those born in the province of Alava and its capital Vitoria-Gasteiz, where pastry chefs compete for excellence in numerous pastelerías (bakeries). In Basque language, a person with a sweet tooth is a gozozale, while something deliciously sweet is called goxua. I omit the traditional sweet syrup here; instead I have added a light raspberry sauce and fun caramel decorations.

Preheat the oven to 190°C/170°C fan/375°F/Gas 5. Grease the cake tin/pan and line with parchment paper.

First, make the sponge. Using an electric hand mixer, whisk the egg whites in a grease-free bowl to form soft peaks. Gradually add the sugar and whisk to a stiff meringue consistency. Using a silicone spatula, fold in the egg yolks, one by one, followed by the flour and vanilla seeds. Pour the batter into the prepared baking tin/pan.

Bake the sponge in the preheated oven for 15 minutes or until the cake is cooked through. Leave to cool completely before removing from the tin. Once cool, cut into rounds to fit your serving glasses.

Meanwhile, prepare the pastry cream. In a saucepan, heat the milk (setting aside a glassful for dissolving the cornflour). Remove the pan from the heat just before the milk starts to boil, then add the vanilla seeds. Cover and leave to infuse for 15 minutes.

Using a metal whisk in a large bowl, beat the egg yolks and sugar together until pale and creamy. In a small bowl, mix the cornflour/cornstarch with the remaining milk. Add to the large bowl, then whisk again. Strain in the infused milk, then whisk again. Return the mixture to the saucepan and heat, stirring continuously, until it thickens. Remove from the heat and leave to cool.

For the caramel decorations, melt the sugar in a pan and cook until it turns an amber colour. Drizzle the caramel onto the parchment paper to make attractive rounds and leave to set.

For the raspberry sauce, place the berries in a pan over a medium heat. Mash the berries to make a coarse sauce. Keep warm.

To assemble, spoon the whipped cream into the bottom of each serving glass, then drizzle over some raspberry sauce. Place a sponge round in each glass, followed by more raspberry sauce and the pastry cream. Top with the caramel decorations.

SPONGE
3 large/US extra-large eggs, separated
80 g/⅓ cup caster/superfine sugar
80 g/⅓ cup plain/all-purpose flour
seeds from ½ vanilla pod/bean

PASTRY CREAM
500 ml/2 cups full-fat/whole milk
seeds from ½ vanilla pod/bean
3 medium/US large egg yolks
70 g/⅓ cup caster/superfine sugar
2 tablespoons cornflour/cornstarch
1 teaspoon caster/superfine sugar

CARAMEL
150 g/¾ cup caster/superfine sugar

RASPBERRY SAUCE
150 g/1¼ cups raspberries

TO SERVE
8 tablespoons double/heavy cream, lightly whipped

30 x 45 cm/12 x 18 inch cake tin/pan

SERVES 6

El pastel de manzana de Silvia
MY GRANDMOTHER SILVIA'S CARAMEL APPLE CAKE

This is a dessert I grew up with. It was cooked by my mother to celebrate family reunions, following the recipe of the best cook in our clan – Silvia, my grandmother. After you have made it once, it will become easier to master. Silvia always used apples of the Reineta variety (Russet family), however I love the firmer texture of the Granny Smith and its lovely acidity. I hope it becomes a celebrated dessert at your dining table, too.

200 g/1 cup caster/superfine sugar
4 medium/US large eggs
100 g/½ cup caster/superfine sugar
500 ml/2 cups full-fat/whole milk
500 g/1 lb. 2 oz. Granny Smith apples
200 g/7 oz. brioche, thinly sliced
single/light cream (optional), to serve

18-cm/7-inch tarte tatin tin/pan or round cake pan/tin, 7 cm/3 inches deep

SERVES 8

First, make the caramel. In a small saucepan, dissolve the sugar in enough water just to cover. Place the pan over a high heat and cook until it turns into an amber coloured caramel – this takes about 5 minutes. Remove the pan from the heat and immediately pour the caramel over the base of the tin/pan – you can reserve a little to serve, if liked. Set aside.

Using an electric hand mixer, beat the eggs with the sugar in a deep mixing bowl until pale and creamy. Using a metal whisk, gradually add the milk, little by little, to make a batter.

Peel and core two apples. Thinly slice the apples. Place the best apple slices in a single overlapping layer over the base of the tin, followed by the remaining apple slices. Dip half of the brioche slices in the batter. Carefully lay the dipped brioche slices on top of the first layer of apples, lightly pressing down with your fingers.

Peel, core and slice the remaining apples as before. Arrange the apple slices in a second layer, followed by a second layer of dipped brioche slices. Pour over any of the leftover batter. Cover the tin with foil, securing well around the rim.

This cake is steamed rather than baked. If you don't have a steamer, place a small bowl upside down in the bottom of a deep saucepan with a tight-fitting lid. Rest the tin on top of the bowl, then carefully pour in enough boiling water to reach just halfway up the tin. Cover the pan with a clean dish towel, followed by the lid of the pan. Lay another dish towel on top of the lid. Gently bring the water to boiling point, then reduce the heat and steam the cake for about 30 minutes. Remove the pan from the heat and leave it still covered with the dish towels and lid until just warm.

Carefully take the tin out of the pan. Invert onto a serving plate, lifting the tin off the cake to unmould. Serve drizzled with reserved caramel and cream for pouring, if you like.

Tejas de almendra de Tolosa
TOLOSA'S ALMOND COOKIES

I simply adore these cookies. You can find tejas (which translates as tiles) throughout Basque Country, even if the people of Tolosa insist theirs are the best. They are equally perfect with an afternoon coffee or following a meal.

75 g/⅓ cup/¾ stick butter,
   at room temperature
200 g/1 cup icing/confectioner's sugar
3 egg whites
40 g/generous ¼ cup plain/
   all-purpose flour
150 g/1½ cups finely ground
   almonds/almond flour
pinch of salt
flaked/slivered almonds, to decorate

MAKES 20

In a mixing bowl, beat the butter with a metal whisk until very creamy. Sift in the sugar and continue beating to incorporate. Next, beat in the egg whites – it will take a few minutes to fully combine these three ingredients. Whisking continuously, sift in the flour, almond flour and salt and beat to a light, creamy consistency.

Preheat the oven to 180°C/160°C fan/350°F/Gas 4. Line a baking sheet with parchment paper.

Working in batches if necessary, place tablespoonfuls of the cookie dough onto the prepared baking sheet, shaping each one into a thin oval, about 9 cm/3½ inches long, making sure they do not touch. Sprinkle the flaked/slivered almonds on top.

Bake the cookies in the preheated oven for about 7 minutes or until the edges of the cookies have taken on a slightly darker colour.

While still warm, carefully remove the cookies from the parchment paper and shape each one around a rolling pin to form a curved tuile. They must be warm to be able to do this, so return any cookies that have cooled down too much to the oven for a few seconds to reheat before shaping.

Index

Acknowledgements

This cookbook is the result of years spent travelling and learning about the food Basque people love and cook. I had the good luck to meet generous home cooks and professional chefs, growers and writers with whom to share a kitchen, a table full or dishes or just a cup of 'café con leche'. Being able to call them my friends is a privilege and a joy. There are too many so let me just mention a few: Pedro, Carmen, Txaro, Joseba, Maite and Palmira.

I am also very grateful to my son Daniel Taylor who has provided some lovely Basque recipes and plenty of advice and to David Swan my husband for his patience and good appetite. They both love Basque food.

Furthermore, this book is also the result of the work of an extensive team of efficient and creative professionals working for Ryland, Peters & Small, a brilliant publishing house determined to defend food and culture from different places in the world. I am very grateful to all of them: Julia Charles, Leslie Harrington, Megan Smith, Abi Waters, Gordana Simakovic, Clare Winfield, Kathy Kordalis, Max Robinson, Lyndon Hayes and Lisa Pendreigh.

Picture credits

All photography by Clare Winfield except on the following pages:
Essay spreads: Pages 14–15 clockwise from top left: María José Sevilla; Fotokon/AdobeStock; neirfy/Adobe Stock; vouvraysan/Adobe Stock; Endika/Adobe Stock; Fernando/Adobe Stock. Pages 16–17 Noradoa/Adobe Stock. Pages 48–49 clockwise from top left: Daniel Meunier/Adobe Stock; grenierb/Adobe Stock; Charo/Adobe Stock. Pages 50–51 Ekaterina Pokrovsky/Adobe Stock. Pages 78–79 clockwise from top left: Clockwise from top left: Ricardo Alvarez Garcia/Alamy Stock Photo; David R. Frazier Photolibrary, Inc./Alamy Stock Photo; Javier Larrea/Alamy Stock Photo; Anadel/ Adobe Stock. Pages 80–81 Kushnirov Avraham/ Adobe Stock. Pages 104–105 clockwise from top left: marcin jucha/Adobe Stock; full image/Adobe Stock; Mariedofra/Adobe Stock. Pages 106–107 Benur/ Adobe Stock. Pages 136–137 clockwise from top left: Jorge Argazkiak/Adobe Stock; txakel/Adobe Stock; Chris Lawrence/Adobe Stock; JuanFrancisco/Adobe Stock; txakel/Adobe Stock; Pavel/Adobe Stock. Pages 138–139 Jorge Argazkiak/Adobe Stock. Pages 164–165 clockwise from top left: Javier Larrea/Alamy Stock Photo; txakel/Adobe Stock; SvetlanaSF/Adobe Stock; Diana Vyshniakova/Adobe Stock; Safi/Adobe Stock. Pages 166–167 AK Media/Adobe Stock.